The Mystery of the Kingdom

Bearing Kingdom Fruit

Steven Lambert, ThD

The Mystery of the Kingdom — Bearing Kingdom Fruit
By Steven Lambert, ThD

© Copyrighted, 1984, 2002; Steven Lambert, ThD.
All rights reserved. No portion of this book may be reproduced in any form or stored by any electronic means without the expressed written consent of the author/publisher.

Scripture quotations, unless otherwise indicated, are taken with the permission from THE NEW AMERICAN STANDARD BIBLE, copyrighted 1977 by the Lockman Foundation. In some cases, special emphasis and explanations have been added by the author.

First Printing — 1984
Second Printing, Revised — 2002

ISBN 1-887915-02-8

Published by:
Real Truth Publications
A Subsidiary of SLM, Inc
P.O. Box 744
Jupiter, FL 33468-0744
Voice: 561- 622-6048 or 624-8096
Fax: 561-776-5973
Administration Email: staff@slm.org
Email Orders: orders@slm.org
Website: http://www.slm.org/pubs/
Online Orders: http://www.slm.org/pubs/orderfrm.html

The Parable of The Sower

Mark 4:1-20

1   And He began to teach again by the seashore. And such a very great multitude gathered before Him that He got into a boat in the sea and sat down; and all the multitude were by the seashore on the land.

2   And He was teaching them many things in parables, and was saying to them in His teaching,

3   "Listen to this! Behold, the sower went out to sow;

4   and it came about that as he was sowing, some seed fell beside the road, and the birds came and ate it up.

5   And other seed fell on the rocky ground where it did not have much soil; and immediately it sprang up because it had no depth of soil.

6   And after the sun had risen, it was scorched; and because it had no root, it withered away.

7   And other seed fell among the thorns, and the thorns grew up and choked it, and it yielded no crop.

8   And other seeds fell into the good soil and as they grew up and increased, they were yielding a crop and were producing thirty, sixty, and a hundredfold."

9   And He was saying, "He who has ears to hear, let him hear."

10   And as soon as He was alone, His followers, along with the twelve, began asking Him about the parables.

11   And He was saying, "To you has been given the mystery of the kingdom of God; but those who are outside get everything in parables,

12   in order that while seeing, they may see and not perceive; and while hearing, they may hear and not understand lest they return again and be forgiven."

13   And He said to them, "Do you not understand this parable? And how will you understand all the parables?

14   The sower sows the word.

15   And these are the ones who are beside the road where the word is sown; and when they hear, immediately Satan comes and takes away the word which has been sown in them.

16   And in a similar way these are the ones on whom seed was sown on the rocky places, who, when they hear the word, immediately receive it with joy;

17   and they have no firm root in themselves, but are only temporary; then, when affliction or persecution arises because of the word, immediately they fall away.

18   And others are the ones on whom seed was sown among the thorns; these are the ones who have heard the word,

19   and the worries of the world, and the deceitfulness of riches, and the desires for other things enter in and choke the word, and it becomes unfruitful.

20   And those are the ones on whom seed was sown on the good ground; and they hear the word and accept it, and bear fruit, thirty, sixty, and a hundredfold."

Contents

Introduction i

Part One: Examining the Parable
Chapter 1: The Paramount Parable 1
Chapter 2: Significance of the Parable 5

Part Two: The Sower And The Seed
Chapter 3: The Sower 11
Chapter 4: The Seed 15

Part Three: The First Category of Hearer
Chapter 5: Those Beside the Road 19

Part Four: The Second Category of Hearer
Chapter 6: Those Like Rocky Ground 21
Chapter 7: Temporary Believers 35
Chapter 8: Affliction and Persecution 43
Chapter 9: Falling Away 51

Part Five: The Third Category of Hearer
Chapter 10: Those With Thorns 69
Chapter 11: Thorn #1: Worries of the World 73
Chapter 12: Thorn #2: Deceitfulness of Riches 81
Chapter 13: Thorn #3: Desires For Other Things 93
Chapter 14: Removing the Thorns 95

Part Six: The Fourth Category of Hearer
Chapter 15: Those With Good Soil 101

Part Seven: The Imperativeness of Bearing Fruit
Chapter 16: The Litmus Test 115
Chapter 17: Consequences of Barrenness 123

Part Eight: Epilogue
Chapter 18: Savior to Judge 131

Introduction

God is in the process of purifying His Church toward the end of glorifying the Eternal Bride of Christ, the Lamb's wife (Rev. 21:9). That is to say, God has already begun to take the Church through a process of *purification unto glorification*, which shall result ultimately in exaltation of the true Bride of Christ unto the final status and station unto which she is destined.

Every former move of God throughout history shall be eclipsed by what is about to take place as God exalts the Church into "all her glory" (Eph. 5:27). And, this thing shall not be done in a corner (Acts 26:26). The entire world shall be made to witness this spectacular phenomenon — the exaltation of a people, a nation, what is called, "A Holy Nation," the Church of the Lord Jesus Christ in all her glory, having no spot or wrinkle or any such thing, a mighty throng, clothed in white garments, girded about with the Truth and the golden breastplate of righteousness, having the high-praises of God in their mouths and a two-edged sword in their hands. While the world, on the other hand, shall be thrust into a chaotic period in which everything that can be shaken, will be, so that in the end all the kingdoms of men shall be toppled.

In the midst of the rubble shall arise another Kingdom — a Kingdom of all majesty and glory — the Kingdom of God.

But, God is even now orchestrating the prelude to this exaltation of the Bride into "all her glory," which is the prerequisite that she be brought into a state of maturity in which she has "no spot or wrinkle or any such thing." To bring her to this state, God has begun to effect a certain kind of judgment of the Church which must precede judgment of the world, for "judgment begins with the Household of God" (1 Pet. 4:17). However, this is not the kind of *punitive* judgment that will come upon the unbelieving world, but rather a judgment for *purging* and *pruning*, a refining judgment, which God long ago foretold He would bring upon the Bride of Christ, the *remnant* of true believers:

> "And it will come about in all the land," declares the Lord, "that two parts in it will be cut off and perish; but the third will be left in it. And I will bring the third part through the fire, refine them as silver is refined, and test them as gold is tested. They will call on My name, and I will answer them; I will say, 'They are my people,' and they will say, 'The Lord is my God.'" (Zec. 13:8,9)

God has already begun to take believers through this refinement process, toward the end that He might reproduce within them the Kingdom of God, that they might bear fruit corresponding to the Life and Kingdom of God, and that they might do the works of Jesus, and greater works in these last days. Indeed, bearing such Kingdom-fruit, as this volume will show, is a Divine requisite for attaining unto Eternal Life and inheriting the Kingdom of God.

Central to this *purification unto glorification* process, is one particular parable of Jesus, the Paramount Parable — the Parable of the Sower. Paramount, because Jesus Himself indicated that understanding this parable was the key to understanding all His other parables concerning the Kingdom of God, and that it contained the very essence of "the mystery of the Kingdom."

Indeed, within this one remarkably ingenious parable is an allegorical revelation, in capsulated form, of the essence of "the mystery of the kingdom," that is, the "secret" of how the Kingdom of God operates and is formed, or reproduced, in the hearts and lives of believers. No other single passage of Scripture so effectively captures and depicts all that is involved in believers bringing forth the fruit of the Kingdom and Life of God in this world.

The Parable of the Sower is paradoxically simple, yet profound. Its meaning is uncomplicated and easily understood. Nevertheless, its import and scope are profound, revealing divine understanding concerning the most vital and essential elements of the Gospel of the Kingdom. As is the the entirety of Scripture, the Parable of the Sower is like the proverbial onion — made up of layer after layer of revelation knowledge — and until perfect knowledge is come (1 Cor. 13:10), no one will fully exhaust its meaning.

In the parable, Jesus delineates four different categories of hearers of the Word of God, which are stereotypical of everyone who has ever heard it. Though each category of hearers heard the Word, it was productive in the lives of only one of the four categories. That is to say that only one category brought forth the fruit that the Word of God is intended and has the innate ability to produce in the lives of earnest and effectual believers. The parable reveals specifically what it was that prevented the first three categories of hearers from bearing the fruit of the Kingdom of God in their own hearts and lives, and what all believers must do to avoid the patterns that produce barrenness.

All things considered, no subject is more central to Christianity, or more vital to Christians.

I truly believe every believer can greatly benefit from a study of this very rich and ingenious parable of Jesus, in which He reveals "the mystery of the Kingdom" of God. In fact, I will take it a step further and say that, based on Jesus' own comments regarding the parable to the early disciples, no disciple of Jesus can expect to understand the Kingdom of God, how it operates, and how to bring forth Kingdom-fruit without understanding this parable.

However, my experience tells me that the vast majority of believers do not grasp many of the truths revealed in this parable. My conviction is that they would be substantially and eternally revolutionized spiritually if they did.

To that end, I earnestly invite you to join me for an in-depth study of the Paramount Parable as our path to understanding "the mystery of the Kingdom."

Part One: Examining the Parable

Chapter One

The Paramount Parable

The parable of the sower, upon which this book is based, may very well be the most important of all the parables of the Lord Jesus Christ. Jesus indicated it was necessary to understand this parable in order to understand all His other parables: "Do you not understand this parable? And how will you understand all the parables?" (Mk. 4:13). This comment demonstrated the importance of this parable.

Why would this particular parable rank above all the others in importance?

Law of Reciprocity

There are two major reasons this parable is so important. The first is that it is based upon one of the most important and fundamental Laws of the Kingdom of God — the Law of Sowing and Reaping, or the Law of Reciprocity. Simply defined, this Law provides that in due season one will reap what he has sown in multiplied return.

God established this Kingdom Law upon the Earth following the great flood at the time of Noah. Promising to never again destroy every living thing and to never again curse the ground, God established the Law of Sowing and Reaping, saying, "While the earth remains, seedtime and harvest...shall not cease" (Gen. 8:21,22).

This Law, however, is not limited to physical procreation, but extends in the spiritual realm to "whatever a man sows, this he will also reap" (Gal. 6:7). So that, a person reaps in kind, according to what he sows. The nature of the harvest, in other words, is determined by the nature of the seed which is sown. The Law will work whether the seed sown is good or bad seed.

Likewise, the amount of the harvest is determined by the amount of the seed sown. It will be a multiplied return directly proportionate to the amount of seed sown: "he who sows sparingly shall also reap sparingly; and he who sows bountifully shall also reap bountifully" (2 Cor. 9:6).

The operation of the entire Kingdom of God is based on this Law of

Sowing and Reaping. God Himself operated this principle in order to reap a bountiful harvest of children born of His Spirit. He sowed His only begotten Son as a Seed. He died a sacrificial death and was buried in the bowels of the earth, planted as a Seed. Concerning this very act, Jesus said of Himself, "Truly, truly, I say to you, unless a grain of wheat falls into the earth and dies, it remains by itself alone; but if it dies, it bears much fruit" (Jn. 12:24).

When the seeds are planted in the ground, however, that is not the end of them, but rather the beginning. They will in due season rise from the ground in multiplied yield.

Praise God, that is exactly the way it happened in the case of Jesus. God sacrificed His only Seed. He died, and His physical body was "buried" in the earth, yet His Spirit descended even deeper into Hell. But, Hallelujah, that was not the end as Satan and his diabolical cohorts thought, it was the beginning. On the third day, He rose again as the "first-fruits" of many brethren. God sowed one Seed, and reaped a multiplied bountiful harvest of Sons of God!

The only way to reap a harvest is to sow some seed. This is the spiritual Law of the Kingdom of God which also governs this earth. As long as the earth remains, this Law will remain in effect.

The key to understanding the parable of the sower, which Jesus said is necessary in order to understand all the other parables concerning the operation of the Kingdom of God, is to remember that everything in the Kingdom operates through this Law of Sowing and Reaping.

Mystery of the Kingdom Revealed

The other reason Jesus ranked this parable of the sower above all the others is that it reveals "the mystery of the Kingdom of God," that is, how the Kingdom of God and its fruit is reproduced in people. This parable, in fact, reveals the step by step formula by which the Kingdom of God is reproduced in believers. After Jesus conveyed the parable, the disciples questioned Him about it because they had not fully understood it. Prefacing His explanation, He said:

> To you has been given the mystery of the kingdom of God; but those who are outside get everything in parables, in order that while hearing, they may hear and not understand lest they return again and be forgiven. (Mk. 4:11,12)

Jesus intimates here that the "mystery of the Kingdom of God" is about to be revealed to the disciples, the *"insiders."* He says that those who are not His disciples were *"outsiders,"* and so they were only given obscure parables. Jesus demonstrated that, when asked, He would, then and now, explain His parables to those who have become true learners and followers, while to those outside the Kingdom they remain enigmatic and incomprehensible conundrums. All of the mystery of the Kingdom of God, you see, is concealed in Christ Jesus (Col. 2:2,3), purposely, and cannot be understood by the unregenerate mind. There is a veil that lies over the carnal mind preventing it from perceiving the Truths of the Kingdom. That veil is only removed in Christ when a person turns to Jesus as his or her Lord: "whenever a man turns to the Lord, the veil is taken away" (2 Cor. 3:14-16).

The principles and precepts of the Kingdom of God are indeed veiled to the unregenerate, and are a mystery to those who are *outside* the Kingdom. But they are in no wise hidden to those *inside* the Kingdom, the true Born Again Children of God, despite the misleading statements of misinformed people based on Old Covenant Scripture to the effect: "Well, you know, God is so mysterious, and His ways are past finding out."

Those dear hearts need to read the *New* Testament, wherein is revealed the Good News that God has made a *new* covenant with the Born Again Children of God, a covenant based on "better promises," in which He reveals the entire mystery of the Kingdom to the beneficiaries.

You see, the New Testament, or New Will, is the revelation of the mystery of the Kingdom of God. A "Testament" is a "will." Once a will has been read, it is no longer "a mystery," that is — "*concealed* knowledge." Then, it is "*revealed* knowledge or Truth." Which is precisely what the New Testament of the Word of God is — the revealed Truth of the Kingdom of God:

> ...the word of God, that is, the mystery, which has been hidden from the past ages and generations; has now been *manifested* to his saints, to whom God **willed** *to make known* what is the riches of the glory of this mystery among the gentiles, which is Christ in you, the hope of glory. (Col. 1:25-27)

Paul says the mystery of the Kingdom of God, which had been hidden from all the previous ages and generations, has now been manifested, or revealed, to the saints, that is to say, believers. He said God Himself "willed" to make even "the riches of the glory of this mystery" known to the saints.

Then, he reveals that the mystery of the Kingdom of God is Jesus Christ Himself, living in the saints. He reiterates that in the second chapter of Colossians, saying, "God's *mystery*, that is *Christ Himself*, in whom are hidden all the treasures of wisdom and knowledge" (Col. 2:2,3).

Praise God, the Will has been read, and the mystery revealed. God has willed to reveal all there is to know about His Kingdom and Himself to His children. As Paul declared, "He made known to us the mystery of His will" (Eph. 1:9). The writers of the New Testament by inspiration of the Holy Spirit have unveiled and revealed to us the mystery, "which in other generations was not made known to the sons of men, as it has now been revealed to His holy apostles and prophets in the Spirit" (Eph. 3:5). The revelation of that mystery is the substance of the New Testament.

In his letter to the Corinthians, Paul speaks of this "mystery" as "God's wisdom," — "the hidden wisdom," which he says is revealed to believers through the Holy Spirit:

> but we speak God's Wisdom in a *mystery, the hidden wisdom*, which God predestined before the ages to our glory; the wisdom which none of the rulers of this age has understood; for if they had understood it, they would not have crucified the Lord of glory; but just as it is written, "Things which eye has not seen and ear has not heard, and which have not entered into the heart of man, all that God has prepared for those who love Him." **For to US God *revealed* them through the spirit**; for the Spirit searches all things, even the depths of God. For who among men knows the thoughts of a man except the spirit of the man, which is in him? Even so the thoughts of God no one knows except the Spirit of God. *Now we have received*, not the spirit of the world, but *the Spirit who is from God*, **that we might KNOW** the things freely given to us by God. (1 Cor. 2:7-2)

God greatly desires to reveal Himself and all of the *"mysteries"* of the Kingdom to true disciples. Those outside the Kingdom will continue to get everything in obscure parables. But, just as Jesus gladly explained the meaning of His parables to the disciples when they asked Him, He will do the same for disciples of today.

The word "disciple" literally means "a learner." If you are willing to learn of Jesus and the *"secrets"* of His Kingdom, He will be willing to teach you. You must be willing to learn in order to receive revelation knowledge of God.

This is precisely what Jesus was doing through the medium of the parable of the sower — giving revelation knowledge concerning the Kingdom of God. In this parable, He unveiled the mystery of the Kingdom of God and how it is reproduced in believers.

All this we have examined in this chapter is some insight as to why this particular parable is so important. In the next chapter we will examine the actual significance of this paramount parable of Jesus.

Chapter Two

Significance of the Parable

The Parable of the Sower is all about bringing forth fruit — fruit of the Kingdom of God, produced from the Seed of the Word of God. That is essentially the significance of this vital parable.

The Word of God is a Seed, the "incorruptible seed" (1 Pet. 1:23), which if sown under the proper conditions will produce the fruit of the Kingdom of God in the lives of those who sow and receive it. The Word of God is the Seed sown by the sower in this parable.

Jesus explained in this parable that there are four basic categories of hearers of the Word of God. Each category heard the Word. The problem was not that they had not heard the Word, for Jesus indicated that each and every category heard the Word. This is a major emphasis of the parable. In His original telling of the parable, Jesus was careful to say that the "seed" was sown upon each category of hearer (see verses 4,5,7,8). Likewise, in His explanation of the meaning of the parable to His disciples, Jesus indicated in each case that the metaphor of the sowing of the seed upon these different categories meant that the Word was preached to them and they heard the Word. Concerning those beside the road, Jesus said, "...and when they hear...the word..." (v. 15). Concerning those who were like rocky places, He said, "...when they hear the Word..." (v. 16). In the case of those who were thorn-infested, He lamented, "these are the ones who have heard the Word..." (v. 18). Then, Jesus distinguished the final category, those who were like good soil, saying, "...they hear the Word and accept it..." (v. 20).

So, all of these people represented in the parable are indeed and indubitably "hearers" (Jas. 1:22) of the Word, and it is vital to keep that in mind when studying this parable and determining its import. They all heard the Word, nevertheless, it was not fruitful in the lives of the first three categories. Only the last category of hearers brought forth fruit. That, in essence, is the proverbial "bottom line" of this powerful and extremely important parable — that only one of the four categories brought forth fruit even though they all had heard the Word of God.

Part of the purpose of the parable was to explain the reasons these people represented by the first three categories of hearers did not bring forth fruit. In so doing, however, Jesus has also ingeniously revealed within the same parable the formula by which a person can successfully bring forth fruit in his or her own life.

Countless multitudes of people have heard the Word of God throughout the ages, including a great portion of the five billion people alive today on planet Earth. Yet, it has been, and is being, fruitful in the lives of only a relatively small few.

It is the highest will of God that His Word bear fruit in the lives of those who hear it. Jesus said every disciple was chosen and appointed for the express purpose "that you should go and bear fruit, and that your fruit should remain" (Jn. 15:16). He said bearing fruit glorified God the Father and proved a person to be a true disciple of Him: "By this is My Father glorified, that you bear much fruit, and so prove to be My disciples" (Jn. 15:8).

Not only is it God's will that those who hear the Word of God bear its fruit in their lives, but, as we will see, bringing forth fruit is a Divine imperative and requirement. James tells us that those who are "hearers only," that is, those who only hear the Word but do not live it, delude or deceive themselves into believing their mere hearing of the Word of God justifies them before God. But, God's Word clearly declares that it is "not the hearers of the Law (Word of God) [who] are just (margin: righteous) before God, but the doers of the Law will be justified" (Rom. 2:13).

Well then, how does a person bear fruit?

Jesus declared the answer to that question:

> Abide in Me, and I in you. As the branch cannot bear fruit of itself, unless it abides in the vine, so neither can you, unless you abide in Me. I am the vine, you are the branches; he who abides in Me, and I in him, he bears much fruit; for apart from Me you can do nothing. (Jn. 15:4,5)

In nature, a branch of a grapevine has no life of its own, but rather it draws its life from the vine itself. A dismembered branch, therefore will eventually and ultimately die.

So it is also in the spiritual realm. Man, in the natural birth, is born into spiritual death. He is alive physically, but dead spiritually. Jesus Christ is the Vine of Life, the Life of God, the essence of Spiritual Life. When a person is Born Again, he is grafted onto the Vine of the Eternal Life of God and thus becomes a spiritually alive branch growing from the Vine of Life. The branch receives its life from the Vine, and in turn bears the fruit which emanates from the Vine. The branch is powerless to produce its own fruit. It only bears the fruit produced by the Vine.

Indeed, Jesus said believers were powerless to bear spiritual fruit by themselves. They must "abide" in Him in order to bear the fruit of the Life of God, for He Himself is the Vine of Life. "Abide in Me, and I in you," He said. The person who does that, "bears much fruit," Jesus promised. That is the only way to bear godly fruit — abide in Jesus, with Him abiding in you. But, how in practicality do we do that — abide in Jesus, and have Him abiding in us?

We do it, first, by being Born Again by inviting Jesus to come and live within our hearts; and, second, by living His Life after He has come in. That is what the word "abide" means — to live. When a person invites Him in, Jesus will come into that person's heart and take up residence there through the Person of the Holy Spirit. Then, with His Life residing within him, that person must then actually live Jesus' Life, or in other words, "abide" in Him.

If we will do these two things, then we will bear much fruit, just as Jesus said. Otherwise, without Him abiding in us and us abiding in Him, Jesus said we can do nothing of spiritual essence or in the way of bearing Godly fruit: "apart from Me you can do nothing." In fact, Jesus went on to say, anyone who does not continue to abide in Him and to manifest His Life, "dries up" spiritually speaking, being separated from the Living Water of the Holy Spirit, and will ultimately be cast into the fires of eternal judgment:

> If anyone does not abide in Me, he is thrown away as a branch, and dries up; and they gather them, and cast them into the fire, and they are burned. (Jn. 15:6)

Thus, we see the absolute imperativeness and essentiality of insuring that we continue to abide in Jesus. So vital, according these texts, is the matter, that the earnest and God-fearing believer is compelled to pose and fervently seek the answer to the question: How then do we know specifically how to "abide" in Jesus, and know with certainty we are indeed living His Life?

Though it may on the surface appear to be too simplistic of an answer to such a critical and consequential question, here is the answer. Jesus Christ was the Word of God (Jn. 1:1). He was the embodiment of the Word of God, the Word of God made flesh, the Word of God personified (Jn. 1:14). He was the incarnate "Word of Life" (1 Jn. 1:1). Jesus was the Living Word of God in a human body. He was the exact and complete representation or manifestation of the Rhema (spoken, manifested) Word and Life of God (Heb. 1:3). That is to say, Jesus was the Living Scriptures.

Moreover, the Bible is the Scripture or Word of God in written form. It contains the written record and revelation of the Life of God, The Eternal Life, the Life of Jesus Christ, who is the First-born genetic Progeny or Son of God, who is also God the Son. Scripture is the written record of the Word of Life, or the Eternal Life, and its substance. Hence, to abide in Jesus, who is the Word of God, is to abide in (obey, manifest, live out) the Word of God, to live the Life revealed, recorded, and represented by the Word of God, i.e., Scripture. To abide in Jesus is to — live the word of God! It is to become "living epistles" "known and read by all men" (2 Cor. 3:2). To abide in Jesus is to become the embodiment and personification of the Word of God after the same manner as Jesus did in His earthly life in human form, though obviously none of us mere mortals, because of the carnal nature that still permeates us, can live His Life with His perfection. Essentially then, to abide in Jesus is to be "DOERS of the word, and not merely hearers only who delude themselves" (Jas. 1:22).

Then, when Jesus is abiding in us and we are abiding in Him, when we are living the Word/Life of God, we will then have the capacity to begin to manifest the fruit of the Kingdom and Life of God in and through our lives. Indeed, we will then be empowered, Jesus said, to "bear much fruit."

Defining "Fruit"

It is important, especially in light of the varied hypotheses that exist concerning the import of the term "fruit," that we define what the "fruit" is that is being spoken of here in our discussion as well as in the passages of Scripture referenced in our discussion. Often preachers anecdotally imply or explicitly state that "fruit" in the Bible refers to people we have led to the Lord, and they sermonize about the "duty" of believers after being saved to lead others to the Lord, often intimating that such "good works" will somehow enhance our standing with God at the final judgment. Aside from the fact that this author does not at all concur with such unScriptural postulations, reasonable and responsible theologians agree that is clearly not the import and application of the term "fruit" as it is used in Scripture.

If we follow one of the foremost rules of Bible interpretation, which is to allow the Bible to interpret the Bible whenever possible, the reasonable conclusion is that the "fruit" spoken of in the Parable of the Sower and the passages cited in our discussions in this book are the attributes of the Nature, Life, or Spirit of God, referred to in Scripture as the "fruit of the Spirit" (Gal. 5:22,23). Namely, the nine "fruit of the Spirit" delineated in these verses are: love, joy, peace, patience, kindness, goodness, faithfulness, gentleness, and self-control. As indicated, they are the attributes of the Nature, Life, or Spirit of God, which we could also describe as the "character" of God.

Thus, true Godly "fruit" then is essentially Godly, or God-like, "character" rather than the so-called "fruit" of those "led to the Lord" and tallied like notches on a gunslinger's six-shooter. In the final judgment, we are going to be judged on the basis of the *quality* of the lives we lived in terms of our faithfulness or obedience to the Word of God, not on the *quantity* of people we have led to the Lord. In other words, our ultimate rewards will be determined by our character, not our "good works." Though true Godly character manifests in outward deeds, its essential eminence over human "good works" lies in the fact that it emanates from the Spirit of God, not from the human nature. These fruit or attributes of the Spirit, by their very nature, are essentially *inward* qualities of God-likeness, or "godliness," which are manifest and expressed in *outward* deeds. They are intrinsically *inward* qualities, but by no means does that mean they are not visible or that they are not manifest outwardly.

Vine's Expository Dictionary of New Testament Words very aptly describes the seeming paradox concerning the metaphorical usage of the term "fruit" in Scriptures as:

> works or deeds, fruit being the visible expression of power working inwardly and invisibly, the character of the fruit being evidence of the character of the power producing it. (Matt. 7:16)

It is saying that the term "fruit" in Scripture refers not to mere inward, invisible abstract mental attitudes or ethereal philosophical concepts, but rather to outward "works" or "deeds" which are indeed real, visible, and tangible. However, those outward works and deeds emanate out of and are produced by the nature and character of God which is inwardly and invisibly resident within the person performing those works and deeds.

To illustrate, in nature, orange trees produce oranges. Oranges are the natural fruit of orange trees. Oranges, though they carry the seed from which orange trees are produced, do not themselves produce oranges. Orange trees produce oranges; oranges don't produce oranges. Oranges have no power to produce oranges; orange trees have the power to produce oranges. Oranges growing on a tree are visible, *outward* evidence that the tree which bears them is an orange tree. The same is true of apples, peaches, pears, grapefruit, cherries, etc. The specie of the tree, that is, its innate nature, is made evident by the fruit it bears. The specie of a tree is not determined by examining its inward parts; nor is a scientific study of its genetic makeup necessary to determine its specie. Rather, the specie of a tree can be readily and easily identified by the fruit it bears outwardly. The fruit a tree bears is outward, visible, and incontrovertible evidence of the innate nature and specie of the tree.

The same is true spiritually. A person's inner essence, Jesus said, can be identified by the fruit he bears outwardly, that is, in his visible deeds: "*the tree is known by its fruit*" (Mat. 12:33). But, He was not speaking of trees, but metaphorically of people. He meant you will be able to identify true believers by whether or not they bear the fruit of the Holy Spirit in their outward deeds. Only those persons who have experienced the regeneration of the New Birth can produce these fruit of spiritual Life, which Life is the Spirit of God, for "*that which is born of the Spirit is Spirit*" (Jn. 3:36). Those experiencing only the natural birth, the birth of the flesh, however, Jesus said, are merely flesh: "*That which is born of the flesh is flesh*" (Jn. 3:6), which abides in death. Thus the natural, carnal man is born into, abides in, and therefore can only manifest the fruit of spiritual death.

Those born of the Divine Nature bear forth the inward attributes of the Holy Spirit in their outward deeds, where it is visible to all. And, Jesus exhorted believers to do just that: "*Let your light shine before men in such a way that they may see your good works*" (Mat. 5:16).

Indeed, the bearing of Godly fruit is the *"litmus test"* of true Christianity, which matter will be discussed in greater detail in Chapter Sixteen after we have examined the Parable itself. The main point established in this chapter, however, is that the bearing of God-like fruit or attributes is the primary significance of the Parable of the Sower.

Now let's take a close-up look at this supremely important and ingenious medium of spiritual Truth — the most important of all Jesus' parables and the parable that reveals "the mystery of the Kingdom of God" — The Parable of the Sower.

Part Two: The Sower and the Seed

Chapter Three

The Sower

Mark 4:3,14
3   Listen to this! Behold, the sower went out to sow;
14 The sower sows the word.

We come now to the parable of the sower itself. The parable consists of three distinct elements: the Seed which is sown, the sower, and the hearers who are the allegorical ground upon which the Seed is sown.

The first element Jesus addresses is the role of the sower, who Jesus identifies as the person who "sows the word." Thus, the sower represents preachers, whose function is to preach the Word of God, sowing it as a Seed. The first thing Jesus does in the parable is to indicate that the sower did his job of sowing the Word, thereby absolving him of all blame for the non-productivity of the Word in the lives of those who did not bear forth fruit after the Seed was sown upon them. Jesus clearly indicates it was not the fault of the sower that these hearers did not bear fruit. The sower did precisely what he was supposed to do, which was to *sow the Word*.

People often want to blame the preacher when those to whom they minister do not grow spiritually and bear fruit. Yet, all the sower can do is to sow the Seed. He can't make it grow. God alone is the one who causes the growth (1 Cor. 3:6). The preacher can only preach it. It is up to the hearers to *accept* and *do* the Word, which, as the parable makes evident, is the very thing that is required for the Seed to become fruitful in the lives of those who hear it.

God-appointed and God-anointed ministers must preach the entire, unadulterated Word of God without compromise, seeking the favor and approval of God, not men, otherwise, they cannot be true bond-servants of God (Gal. 1:10). God instructs all ministers: "Study to show thyself approved unto God, a workman that needeth not to be ashamed, rightly dividing the word of truth" (2 Tim. 2:15, KJV).

Moreover, the spiritual role of God's messengers is to be wholly devoted to prayer and the ministry of the Word (Acts 6:4), not spending the vast majority of their time as business administrators, social affairs coordinators, recreation directors, and merely the proverbial "shoulder to cry on." As much as is possible and practical, they should immerse themselves in prayer and the ministry of the Word, rather than expending their efforts and energies on spiritually unproductive and inconsequential activities. God's highest will is that His appointed ministers be supported by those to whom they minister, enabling them to "get their living from the gospel" (1 Cor. 9:14), and thereby be wholly dedicated to their calling, for:

> No soldier in active service entangles himself in the affairs of everyday life, so that he may please the one who enlisted him as a soldier. (2 Tim. 2:4)

God's chosen ministers are commanded to preach the Word in season and out, to reprove, rebuke, exhort, and instruct the Flock of God (2 Tim. 4:2). All these things are both their function and responsibility to the Body of Christ, which they are required to faithfully discharge. They must preach, reprove, rebuke, exhort, and instruct on the basis of the Word, despite the fact we are now in the time concerning which God foretold:

> The time will come when they will not endure sound doctrine; but wanting to have their ears tickled, they will accumulate for themselves teachers in accordance to their own desires; and will turn away their ears from the truth, and will turn aside to myths. (2 Tim. 4:3,4)

This is precisely what many congregations do today — "accumulate for themselves" by democratic election (a totally unScriptural procedure) "teachers in accordance to their own desires" who will only tickle the ears of their "electors," preaching only what they want to hear, turning away from the Truth of God's Word unto spiritual myths and erroneous doctrines. Moreover, we have entirely too many cowardly "hirelings" filling the pulpits of our churches today who are willing to cowtow to the wishes of the people, who, in order to keep their job, preach only the stereotypical denominational doctrines and only what the "people-ruled" church wants to hear.

The Church of which the Lord Jesus Christ is the Head, however, is not a democracy, operating on the basis of a satanically inspired, humanistic order of people-rule. No, the true Church is a Theocracy, operating on the basis of the Headship of Christ and the order of Divine Authority, and is God-ruled. The Church is not operated according to *Roberts' Rules of Order*, but according to God's Rules of Order. God Himself appoints and anoints the ministers of His Church (1 Cor. 12:28), and He does not ask for anyone to "second" His motions.

Jesus charged the Apostle Peter, who He Himself had chosen and appointed, "feed My sheep" as validation of the love Peter thrice emphatically asserted he had for Jesus. That incident made an indelible impression on Peter, for he himself later exhorted other under-shepherds of the Chief Shepherd to:

> shepherd (feed) the flock of God among you, exercising oversight not under compulsion, but voluntarily, according to the will of God; and not for sordid gain, but with eagerness. (1 Pet. 5:2)

It is the high calling of God-appointed ministers to devote themselves to prayer and the ministry of the Word of God, and to in turn feed the Flock of God with the Bread of Life, the Word of God. God has chosen and appointed them for this very purpose. Jesus Himself is the Chief Shepherd (1 Pet. 5:4), the Head of the Church, but He entrusts the care of His Flock to the ministers He appoints. He entrusts to them the responsibility of shepherding and feeding His sheep, primarily by sowing the Word into their lives. Those occupying shepherdship positions who do not heed those instructions are forewarned with this poignant admonition:

> Woe, shepherds...who have been feeding themselves! Should not the shepherds feed the flock? You eat the fat and clothe yourselves with the wool, you slaughter the fat sheep without feeding the flock. Those who are sickly you have not strengthened, the diseased you have not healed, the broken you have not bound up, the scattered you have not brought back, nor have you sought for the lost; but with force and with severity you have dominated them. And they were scattered for lack of a shepherd....Thus says the Lord God, "Behold, I am against the shepherds, and I shall demand My sheep from them and make them cease from feeding sheep. So the shepherds will not feed themselves anymore, but I shall deliver My flock from their mouth, that they may not be food for them." (Ezk. 34:2-10)

As Jesus so succinctly put it in the Parable of the Sower, "the sower sows the Word." Thus, the Word of God is the Seed the sower sows.

Let us examine now this Seed which the sower sows.

Chapter Four

The Seed

Mark 4:14
14 The sower sows the Word.

Jesus identifies the Seed sown by the sower in the parable as being the Word of God. Indeed, the Word of God is "the incorruptible seed" (1 Pet. 1:23). Essentially, this means that the innate efficacy of the Word of God as the Seed of the Life of God cannot be in any way corrupted, perverted, or degenerated. This only stands to reason because the Seed of the Word of God is Jesus Himself, who is the Son of God and God the Son (1 Jn. 1:1-14; Jn. 1:1-3). Therefore, just as the sower cannot be faulted for the Word not becoming fruitful in the lives of the first three categories of hearers, neither was their fruitlessness due to some fault or deficiency of the Seed which the sower sowed because that Seed is the perfect Son of God, the Christ Himself, the very Life of God.

In no way can any culpability whatsoever for the barrenness of the first three categories of hearers be attributed to the Seed that was sown by the sower. God Himself solemnly testifies He is personally watching over His Word in order to perform it (Jer. 1:12). He also said His Word shall not return unto Him void (i.e., fruitless), but that it will unfailingly accomplish the purpose for which it was sent (Is. 55:11). In other words, God guarantees His Word will *perform* exactly what it *promises*. When applied with faith and perseverance, God's Word will perform exactly what it promises, every time, in every situation, in every facet of life. As the Apostle Paul said, "the word of truth...is constantly bearing fruit and increasing" (Col. 1:5,6). As both Joshua and Solomon said, "not one word has failed of all His good promise" (1 Kgs. 8:56).

It is impossible for the Word of God to fail. Whenever, wherever, and with whomever it seems the promises of the Word of God are not being performed, the reason can never be any deficiency with the Word of God or God Himself. Indeed, it is absolutely indisputable that the reason the first three categories of hearers do not bear fruit in their lives is not because of any deficiency on the part of either the sower or the Seed. Rather, as we will see in the succeeding chapters, it is the condition of the soil of the hearers' hearts and what they do with the incorruptible Seed of the Word of God that determines whether or not the Word will bear fruit in their lives.

The Holy Spirit reveals through the Apostle James some very crucial information regarding the salvation or sanctification of our souls:

> Therefore putting aside all filthiness and all that remains of wickedness, in humility receive the Word implanted, which is able to save your souls. But prove yourselves doers of the word, and not merely hearers who delude themselves. (Jas. 1:21)

The import of this passage is that we must "receive" the Word of God by allowing it to be "implanted" as "the incorruptible seed" of the Life of God in the good soil of an obedient heart, and be a "doer" of the Word rather than a mere "hearer," in order for it to be "able" to perform its task of "saving" our soul. Now it is important to understand that the word "save" in this verse, which is used more than a hundred times in the New Testament, is the word "sozo" in the original language, which means to restore to the original condition, to make whole, to make holy. Essentially, the word speaks of restoring us to the original state of wholeness and holiness in which Man (Adam) was created and had prior to the fall into perdition, as opposed to the traditional concept of the import of the word "saved," the primary emphasis of which is that those who are "saved" will go to Heaven after they die or at the rapture if they remain alive when Jesus returns.

It is also vital to note that the text explicitly refers to the salvation or sanctification of our "souls" which the Word is able to accomplish when we receive it implanted. Having been created in the Image of the Triune God, Man is a tripartite being, meaning the human essence consists of three parts, which are: spirit, soul, and body (1 Thes. 5:23). When a person receives Jesus and is Born Again, it is into his or her heart, i.e., spirit, that Jesus is received and takes up residence, and it is the spirit which is regenerated or restored to holiness and wholeness, for: "that which is born of the Spirit is (*the human*) spirit" (Jn. 3:6, italics added by author).

As indicated in James 1:21, the *soul*, however, which consists of the mind, will, and emotions, is **not** instantaneously saved or sanctified at the New Birth. Rather, the saving or sanctifying of the *soul* is a protracted, progressive, ongoing process which transpires over the course of one's life subsequent to the New Birth. So, while our *spirit* is instantaneously saved and sanctified at the New Birth, our *soul*, or mind, will, and emotions, is not. It is as we receive the Word of God implanted into those parts of our being — our thinking, our desires, and our feelings — that our *soul* is progressively saved and sanctified, commensurate to the degree to which we "receive" the concepts of the Word of God into these areas of our lives and become conformed to them.

Hence, we have seen then the specific role and absolute reliability of the Seed of the Word of God in the Parable of the Sower, and that it can in no wise be blamed for the failure of the first three categories of hearers to bring forth fruit after it was sown into their lives.

Thus far, we have laid the groundwork necessary for examining this very rich parable. We come now to the real "meat" of the parable — the four categories of hearers of the Word of God. Though each category heard the Word, only the last category of hearers brought forth fruit. We examine them to see the reasons that was so.

Part Three: The First Catgory of Hearer

Chapter Five

Those Beside the Road

Mark 4:4,15
4   and it came about that as he was sowing, some seed fell beside the road, and the birds came and ate it up.
15   And these are the ones who are beside the road where the word is sown; and when they hear, immediately Satan comes and takes away the word which has been sown in them.

The first category of hearers of the Word Jesus discussed in this parable is — "the ones who are beside the road." He characterized them as being "beside the road" because according to verse fifteen they rejected the Word when they heard it, and thus remained beside the road of Eternal Life, unsaved. Luke's account of the same parable makes this even more evident that "those beside the road" represents the unbelieving and unsaved:

> And those beside the road are those who have heard; then the devil comes and takes away the word from their heart, so that they may not believe and be saved. (Lk. 8:12)

Like all the other categories of hearers, this category did hear the Word. Sowers of the Word indeed sow it upon those who are beside the road, the unsaved, exhorting them to accept the Gospel and to receive Jesus. Praise God that the Word *is* sown on those beside the road, otherwise no one would ever be saved.

But, the hearts of these hearers were hardened against the Word, so they rejected it and the Savior it preaches. Consequently, the Seed remained on the surface of the hard ground of their hearts, making it prey to Satan's evil birds who came to snatch it all up.

In other words, when the Seed of the Word was not "received implanted" (Jas. 1:21) in the good soil of acceptance (Mk. 4:20), Satan dispatched his evil spirits, which Jesus figuratively referred to as "birds," to snatch it all up. As Jesus indicated, just as soon as they hear the Word without receiving it, "immediately, Satan comes and takes away the word which has been sown in them" (Mk. 4:15). He does this to prevent the hearer from being able to meditate upon the Word any further, and thus preclude any subsequent acceptance of it.

The "road" in the parable which these people were beside is the "road" of Eternal Life. There is only one "road" or "way" to Heaven.

Jesus Christ is *the* Way, *the* Truth, and *the* Eternal Life; no one comes to the Father except by Him (Jn. 14:6, italics added by author). His Life, resident within and manifest through true believers is the only thing that makes them acceptable unto God and for attaining unto the glory of Heaven: "Christ in you, the hope of glory" (Col. 1:27). This first category of hearers, however, rejected the Word, and thus remained beside the road of Eternal Life — lost and undone without God.

Jesus is the Way to Heaven and eternal fellowship with God. He is the gate unto Eternal Life, "and few are those who find it" (Mt. 7:14), even though the call to salvation is extended to "whoever will call upon the name of the Lord" (Rom. 10:13). Salvation is a free gift to all those who will accept the Gospel as they hear it, and believe upon the Lord Jesus Christ, receiving Him as Savior and Lord.

Now, there is another way, a way that seems right unto man, but the final destination of which is death and destruction (Pr. 14:12; 16:25). The people of the world who refuse to repent and receive the Gospel of Salvation travel this broad and wide, no restraints, licentious, "everything goes" road. But, unfortunately, it leads straight to Hell's unquenchable fires of eternal judgment (Mat. 7:13). The only "exit ramp" off that road is the Lord Jesus Christ.

It is a Life or death matter that every hearer of the Word accept and obey it, and thereby get up on the road of Eternal Life, instead of remaining beside it. Hearing alone is not enough. Every hearer must fully accept the Word, receive it implanted, and get up on the road of Eternal Life by obeying it.

This is the first step to bringing forth the fruit of Eternal Life and the Kingdom of God.

Part Four
The Second Category of Hearer

Chapter Six

Those Like Rocky Ground

Mark 4:5,6,16,17
5   And other seed fell on the ROCKY GROUND where it did not have much soil; and immediately it sprang up because it had no depth of soil.
6   and after the sun had risen, it was scorched; and because it had no root, it withered away.
16   And in a similar way these are the ones on whom seed was sown on the rocky places, who, when they hear the word, immediately receive it with joy;
17   and they have no firm root in themselves, but are only temporary; then, when affliction or persecution arises because of the word, immediately they fall away.

This portion of Jesus' parable concerns the second category of hearers, who Jesus allegorically described as "rocky ground." He indicated that the Word was not fruitful in the lives of these hearers because their hearts were like "rocky ground."

Next to the seed itself, the most important element in agriculture is the soil. The soil is what the seed is actually implanted in. It is the incubator, or "womb," if you will, in which the seed undergoes its gradual metamorphosis unto life. There are two factors regarding the condition of the soil that are crucial to successful crop production. The first one is the fertility and condition of the soil, and the other is the depth of the soil. There must be sufficient depth of soil to foster the development of a root system adequate to sustain the crop all the way through its development to full maturity. Otherwise, the crop will die before reaching maturity and fruition.

Jesus revealed in verse five of our text that not enough depth of soil was precisely the problem in the case of this category of hearers. Because the ground was "rocky ground" — "it did not have much soil." It did have *some* soil, enough to receive the seed implanted, but not enough to foster the development of a root system adequate to sustain the proper growth of the plant unto full maturity.

The root system of a plant is its "umbilical cord." The plant is wholly dependent upon the root system to supply vital nutrients it absorbs from within the earth. It can only grow proportionate to the extensiveness and effectiveness of the roots. The deeper and broader the roots extend, the more water and nutrients it can supply to the plant. The more water and nutrient it supplies, the more developed and fruitful will be the plant.

Moreover, it is during the hot, arid summer months, when the sun's rays are at their peak intensity, that the plant's dependence on the root system is at its maximum. Water in the surface soil soon diminishes. The root system must then draw water from deep within the ground to keep the plant from being scorched.

But, this ground was "rocky ground." The soil was shallow because of rocks underneath. Therefore, the crop "had no root," Jesus said (v. 6). Thus, "after the sun had risen, it was scorched." It was scorched because there was not an adequate root system to supply the plant with sufficient water to survive the intense heat of the sun. Consequently, "it withered away" before it could grow to the fruit-bearing stage of full maturity.

Jesus indicated in verse five that there was *some* initial growth, however, prior to it withering away: "and immediately it sprang up." There was some growth, but in the end it proved to be futile, since the plant subsequently withered away prior to maturing to the stage in which it could bear fruit.

The Explanation

When Jesus began to explain this portion of the parable to His disciples, He said this whole scenario was representative of people on whom the seed of the Word of God is sown whose hearts are like "rocky places, who, when they hear the word, immediately receive it with joy." In others words, their initial response to the Word was to receive it joyfully, which seems good. However, what was not readily visible was the fact that their hearts were still full of rocks, which would eventually be their downfall.

What did the rock represent? Rock is characteristically hard and unyielding. Thus, it symbolizes hardened, unyielding disobedience of the Word. Being likened unto "rocky ground," indicated that there was still a lot of the "heart of stone" (Ezk. 36:26) remaining in these hearers' lives, which represents disobedience to God and resistance of His Word.

In contrast to the rock, the soil, with its pliant and yielding nature, represents acceptance and obedience of the Word. Jesus gave a clue to that in His description of the last category of hearers, who He likened unto "good soil" because they *accepted* the Word when they heard it and thus bore fruit, "thirty, sixty, and a hundredfold" (Mk. 4:20).

Further evidence that the soil represents acceptance of the seed of the Word is found in a passage alluded to before: "receive the Word implanted, which is able to save your souls" (Jas. 1:21). As mentioned before, it is the soil that receives the seed implanted. To *receive* something is to *accept* it.

The shallow layer of top soil these people had, therefore, represented a superficial acceptance of the Word. They had enough initial acceptance of the Word to "receive the Word implanted," and thus to be saved. The initial growth Jesus described by saying, "and immediately it sprang up," was further evidence that these people were saved and had begun Eternal Life.

This did favorably distinguish this second category of hearers from the first, in that the first category rejected the Word entirely when they heard it. Thus, they remained unsaved, "beside the road" of Eternal Life. The "rocky grounders" did receive the seed implanted, and were saved. Then, as the Life cycle progressed, the seed began to undergo its metamorphosis unto life. Their root system began to grow and extend downward as the Word says is necessary: "Let your roots grow down into Him (Jesus) and draw up nourishment from Him" (Col. 2:7, L.B.). But, as the roots grew deeper, they soon reached the rock which lay hidden beneath the surface soil. The rock obstructed the root, preventing it from extending any further. So, then, when the roots could grow no deeper, the stalk of the plant began to grow upward above the ground: "and immediately it sprang up because it had no depth of soil."

But, the underdeveloped root system could not supply ample water and nutrient for the plant to endure against the elements and continue growing unto maturity. Soon it withered and died.

What did all this mean?

Insufficient Repentance

Allegorically, what all this that Jesus was saying here meant was that these people had not made a complete repentance in their lives and thereby removed all of the rocks of sin that were present deep within their soul, hidden beneath the superficial layer of soil, which we established typified repentance. Rather, their repentance was only superficial and insufficient to allow the root system to extend as deep as was necessary for the plant to survive the scorching heat of the sun. Thus, "after the sun had risen, it was scorched; and because it had no root, it withered away."

Now these "rocky grounders" obviously did do some repenting, as evidenced by the fact that they at least had sufficient topsoil in which to "receive the Word implanted" (Jas. 1:21), which certainly was good and commendable as a first step. However, the problem was that their repentance was only that — superficial, and not deep enough. The reason Jesus described these people as being like "rocky ground" is that even though they did have some top-soil, beneath that superficial layer of soil there still remained rocks of rebellion and sin, and disobedience of God's Word and general revealed Will. Hence, Jesus was indicating here that this category of believers only repented of the conspicuous "surface sins," but not of the attitudinal sins that lied deeper within their inner-being and which were not so readily visible to others.

First Word of the Gospel

Repentance is an absolute imperative and the initial prerequisite of true salvation and complete sanctification. It is the very foundation of the Gospel, as this phrase in Hebrews 6:1 indicates: "...a foundation of repentance...." In other words, "repent" is the first word of the Gospel of Jesus Christ.

Indeed, it was the first word of the Gospel that John The Baptist preached: "Now in those days John the Baptist came, preaching in the wilderness of Judea, saying, '*repent*, for the kingdom of heaven is at hand'" (Mat. 3:1,2, italics added by author).

It was the first word of the Gospel that Jesus preached: "From that time Jesus began to preach and say, '*repent*, for the kingdom of heaven is at hand'" (Mat. 4:17, italics added by author). In fact, Jesus bluntly and explicitly preached that everyone must repent or they would all perish: "Unless you *repent*, you will all likewise perish" (Lk. 13:3,5, italics added by author).

"Repent" was also the first word and essence of the Gospel preached by the original twelve Apostles of the Lamb who Jesus personally trained, commissioned, and sent out: "And He summoned the twelve and began to send them out in pairs....And they went out and preached that men should *repent*" (Mk. 6:7-12, italics added by author).

After the same manner, Jesus also commissioned the entire Church to preach that people must repent in order to receive forgiveness of their sins unto salvation:

> ...and He said to them, "Thus it is written, that the Christ should suffer and rise again from the dead the third day; and that *repentance* for forgiveness of sins should be proclaimed in His name to all the nations, beginning from Jerusalem." (Lk. 24:46,47, italics added by author)

The Apostle Peter, after his own falling away and subsequent restoration and empowerment from on High by means of the promised Immersion in the Holy Spirit on the Day of Pentecost, forthrightly proclaimed in his now infamous first sermon that repentance is the initial required response to the true Gospel of Christ, and a mandatory prerequisite for whosoever desires to receive forgiveness of sins and the infilling of, as well as the Immersion in, the Holy Spirit:

> Now when they heard this, they were pierced to the heart, and said to Peter and the rest of the apostles, "Brethren, what shall we do?" And Peter said to them, "*repent*, and let each of you be baptized in the name of Jesus Christ for the forgiveness of your sins; and you shall receive the gift of the Holy Spirit." (Acts 2:37,38, italics added by author)

Peter also declared that a person must be willing to fully repent of all acts and attitudes of sin and to return to God in order to truly receive remission of the guilt and penalty of sin, and receive Jesus into his heart:

> *Repent* therefore and return, that your sins may be wiped away, in order that times of refreshing may come from the presence of the Lord; and that He may send Jesus, the Christ appointed for you. (Acts 3:19,20, italics added by author)

There simply is no salvation without repentance. Repentance is the Divine imperative to receiving Eternal Life:

> And when they heard this, they quieted down, and glorified God, saying, "Well then, God has granted to the Gentiles also the repentance that leads to (*Eternal*) life." (Acts 11:18, italics added by author)

What Then Is Repentance?

Now if all this concerning repentance is so, and it is, then it certainly is imperative that we all have a thorough and accurate understanding of what repentance is. The word "repent" literally means to have a change of mind which results in a resolute decision to turn from going in one direction, turn around, and go in the opposite direction. Repentance is not merely an intention, or a desire, or an emotion, but rather an act. As it has been said: "the road to Hell is paved with good *intentions*." And, so often, people somehow genuinely believe they should be judged based on their *intentions*, though they judge others on the basis of their deeds. But, repentance is not what you intend to do; it is not real repentance until you have done it.

True repentance is not just some determinate resolution, like those made by people of the world at New Years. Neither is it mere reformation, that is, "turning over a new leaf," as people often resolve. Such self-willed resolves and outward reformation, even if successful, can never bring anyone into fellowship and rightstanding with God. True repentance, instead, is the act of turning away from every form and appearance of evil and turning unto God, not by the might and power of self-will and self-discipline, but by the empowerment of the Holy Spirit (Zec. 4:6). It means to turn around from following after "the course of this world" (Eph. 2:2), in order to follow after the course of Eternal Life. True repentance is the act of turning away from sin and self, and turning unto God in complete surrender and subjection of one's entire being — spirit, soul, and body — unto God and His Word unto the accomplishment of His Will via His Ways.

Repentance is not remorse. Repentance and remorse are not synonymous, though many people think they are. Remorse, no matter how intense and sincere, is only an emotion. True repentance, on the other hand, is not merely an emotion, or a *feeling*, but a deliberate, decisive, and definite *deed*. Remorse is something you *feel*; repentance is something you *do*.

Now this is not to say, however, that remorse does not serve any purpose. On the contrary, remorse is a powerful motivating force of the conscience of man which even in the natural keeps those who are guided by a basic sense of propriety and decency from engaging in patently improper and injurious behavior. However, simply feeling remorseful does not itself constitute true repentance. Many people feel remorseful for misdeeds and sin they have committed, but that remorse does not always cause them to repent and cease from engaging in that wrongful conduct.

Moreover, there is a genuine remorse, a "godly sorrow," which is "according to the will of God," which is the working of the Holy Spirit to convict people of their sin, and which is a precursor and motivation unto true and effectual repentance. If those who are under that conviction and "godly sorrow" of the Holy Spirit will but yield to it, it will lead them to true repentance without remorse, which in turn leads to true salvation:

> For though I caused you sorrow by my letter, I do not regret it; though I did regret it — for I see that the letter caused you sorrow, though only for a while — I now rejoice, not that you were made sorrowful, but that you were made sorrowful according to the will of God....For the sorrow that is according to the will of God produces a *repentance without regret* (remorse), leading to salvation; but the sorrow of the world produces death. For behold what earnestness this very thing, this Godly sorrow has produced in you....(2 Cor. 7:8-11, italics added by author)

Superficial Repentance

As alluded to earlier, to their credit, these "rocky grounders" apparently did at least comply with the requirements of the Gospel to the extent of effecting some superficial repentance, whether acquiescently or enthusiastically. We know this based on Jesus' description of this category of hearers' eventual course. In verse five of the text, He said those who were like "rocky ground...did not have much soil," and that they "had no depth of soil." He did not say they didn't have *any* soil, only that they did not have *much* and that what they did have had "no depth." Indeed, they did have enough soil, which we established symbolized acceptance of and compliance with the Word of God, to initially receive the seed of the Word of God implanted (Jas. 1:21), for Jesus said "when they hear the word, (they) immediately receive it with joy" (Mk. 4:16).

Moreover, because the Word of God is the ever-living and abiding "incorruptible seed" (1 Pet. 1:23-25) which lives forever and cannot cease to live, and which is "constantly bearing fruit and increasing" (Col. 1:6), it did spring up, according to what Jesus said, "and immediately it sprang up because it had no depth of soil" (Mk. 4:5), even though the soil of these hearers in which the seed of the Word was implanted was shallow and had no depth. But, this testifies more of the efficacy and virility of the Word of God than it does of anything meritorious in the receivers.

Jesus was saying allegorically here that there was a certain amount of initial spiritual development of the stalk of the plant above the ground, which gave the false and deceptive appearance of legitimacy and normalcy, and that it would in time develop and bear fruit. However, ultimately, that would all prove to be untrue, because "after the sun had risen, it was scorched; and because it had no root, it withered away" before it could fully develop to the fruit-bearing stage of full maturity and bear forth fruit.

As is always the case, Jesus carefully and deliberately chose each word He spoke in this parable. Thus, by saying, "immediately it sprang up," He was subtly hinting about these "plants" growing in "God's field" (1 Cor. 3:9) what every farmer or even amateur gardener knows — that when a plant springs up faster than normal, that is not a good, but a very ominous sign. It is an indication that something is wrong with the development of that plant, because the initial and most important part of the development of any plant is the development of its root system, which is its downward and invisible development. Whereas, the upward and visible development of the plant, which occurs above the ground must only take place after an adequate root system has developed.

As we have already firmly established, the superficial layer of soil within these hearers' hearts, into which the seed of the Word was implanted, represented superficial repentance. Beneath this superficial layer of top-soil, there still remained rocks of disobedience and sin which they had not removed. These rocks of unyieldedness to God and the principles of His Kingdom were irrefutable evidence that their repentance was only superficial. The primary point Jesus was emphasizing with regard to these "rocky grounders" was that as zealous as they may appear to be at first, they would eventually fall away from the faith, and the primary cause of their eventual apostasy was that their repentance was only superficial.

Unfortunately, there are many people who are of this ilk, who Jesus described as "those with rocky ground," who have no depth of repentance. They are willing to repent of the outward, "surface sins," such as smoking, drinking, and cursing, and some of this category are even willing to go as far as to repent of some of the more obvious and conspicuous sins of the flesh such as immorality, impurity, sensuality, carousing (partying), and the like, which is all well and good. But, there is more to the complete repentance which God desires of believers. He wants and even requires more than mere *superficial* repentance. As King David wrote in repentance and contrition after finally coming to his right senses and coming under conviction concerning his sin, God desires (and what He desires, He requires) uprightness and integrity in our *heart*: "thou dost desire truth in the innermost being, and in the hidden part Thou wilt make me know wisdom" (Ps. 51:6).

Inward Repentance

You see, all sin is preeminently of the heart, the inward man, the "innermost being" and "hidden part" as David referred to it. Sin can be aptly defined as inward attitudes of rebellion which are expressed in outward deeds. Sin is rebellion against God's Laws. It is disobedience of God's Word. Moreover, all sin, whether it exists in the form of inward attitudes or whether it has found expression in outward deeds, causes a breach in fellowship with God, and spiritually defiles the offender.

But, the point that must be emphasized is that before sin finds expression in outward deeds, it first begins in the heart in the form of a rebellious attitude. And, it is actually these inward attitudes of rebellion that defile a person spiritually, whether or not they are ever expressed in outward speech and deeds, as Jesus Himself revealed in the following passage:

> But the things that proceed out of the mouth come from the heart, and those defile the man. For out of the heart come evil thoughts, murders,

adulteries, fornications, thefts, false witness, slanders. These are the things which defile the man. (Mat. 15:18-20a)

"The *things*" which Jesus described in this passage are inward attitudes of the heart. He said it was these attitudes in the "innermost being" that actually spiritually defile a person. His point here was that it is not really the expression of these iniquities in outward speech and deeds that defile people spiritually, but rather the inward rebellious attitudes from which they are generated.

It is from these inward attitudes of rebellion that we all must repent in order to make a complete surrender unto God. We must go beyond superficial repentance to inward repentance, turning away not only from the obvious and conspicuous sins of commission, but also from the inward attitudes of sin in our "hidden part," which though they are not always as readily visible to the eyes of men, they are always plainly visible to God. While Abraham Lincoln's famous quip may be true — "You can fool some of the people all of the time, and all the people some of the time, but you can't fool all the people all of the time" — the fact of the matter remains we cannot fool God at all, anytime. He sees it all, for "there is no creature hidden from His sight, but all things are open and laid bare to the eyes of Him with whom we have to do" (Heb. 4:13).

Pure Hearts

Does God really require inward as well as outward repentance?

The answer is: Yes, He does. As already mentioned, David said to God, "Behold, Thou dost desire truth in the innermost being" (Ps. 51:6). The "innermost being" of a person is his spirit, or heart. The Triune God created Man in His own Image as a *tripartite* being, that is, consisting of three parts: spirit, soul, and body. Like God, Man was created preeminently a spirit-being; we **are** a *spirit*, we **have** a *soul* (mind, will, and emotions), and we **live** in a physical *body*. That is what we all are. Man's *spirit* is his "innermost being," or what is also called his *heart*, which does not refer to the anatomical organ inside our chest that pumps our blood. The words "spirit" and "heart" are used interchangeably in the Bible.

When the totality of Scripture is considered, it becomes unmistakably clear and irrefutable that God does indeed desire and even require that believers have pure hearts, having repented of both inward and outward sin. Indeed, even though such a statement is a definite departure from modern liberal theology, I will nevertheless even go so far as to state categorically that having a heart purified by the shed blood of the Lamb and the miraculous, supernatural sanctifying power of the Holy

Spirit is a requirement for being granted entrance into the Portals of Heaven:

> Who may ascend into the hill of the Lord (*Heaven*)? And who may stand in His holy place (*Heaven*)? He who has clean hands (*outward deeds*) and a pure heart.... (Ps. 24:3,4, italics added by author)

The Apostle Paul summarized the goal of the instruction of the entire New Testament as: "love from a pure heart and a good conscience and a sincere faith" (1 Tim. 1:5). Furthermore, he also exhorted:

> Therefore, if a man cleanses himself from **these things** (*unrighteous and lawless conduct he had enumerated*), he will be a vessel for honor, sanctified, useful to the Master, prepared for every good work. Now flee from youthful lusts, and pursue righteousness, faith, love, and peace, with those who call on the Lord from a pure heart. (2 Tim. 2:21,22)

Jesus Himself taught that the "pure in heart" were blessed and were the ones that would "see God" (Mat. 5:8).

James commanded, "Cleanse your hands, you sinners," speaking of repentance of sinful outward deeds, and "purify your hearts, you double-minded," speaking of **inward** *repentance* (Jas. 4:8).

God's Part: Sanctification

Repentance is our part of the bargain, so to speak. God requires that we turn away from serving Satan to serve Him, that we turn away from sin unto purity and holiness. But as we do that, there is another process the Holy Spirit begins to effect in the lives of believers. That process is called — "sanctification." Simply defined, sanctification, as the literal meaning of the Greek word so translated connotes, is the process of being made holy. It is the working of the Holy Spirit to bring the believer into obedience of Jesus Christ: "...by the sanctifying work of the Spirit, that you may obey Jesus Christ and be sprinkled with His blood" (1 Pet. 1:2).

No one has the power or ability to sanctify *himself*, even by the most determinate and willful efforts. Sanctification is not self-discipline, though self-discipline is essential and necessary. Sanctification, however, is effected solely through the residency of the Life of Jesus Christ, the Holy Spirit, in the heart and life of the believer:

> But by His doing you are in Christ Jesus, who became to us wisdom from God, and righteousness and SANCTIFICATION, and redemption, that, just as it is written, "Let him who boasts, boast in the Lord." (1 Cor. 1:30,31)

Sanctification and its fruit — holiness — is a mandatory prerequisite for entrance into Heaven and eternal fellowship with God: "Pursue peace with all men, and the sanctification ("holiness," KJV) without which no one will see the Lord" (Heb. 12:14).

Some people balk at the premise that God requires holiness of believers. Nevertheless, holy behavior most certainly is a requisite for true Born Again children of God:

> As obedient children, do not be conformed to the former lusts which were yours in your ignorance, but like the Holy One who called you, **be Holy yourselves** also in all your behavior; because it is written, **"you shall be Holy**, for I am Holy." (1 Pet. 1:14-16)

God is a Holy God. The Divine Nature, or the Holy Spirit, consists of pristine and perfect Holiness. That's the reason the Spirit of God is called "the Holy Spirit." In his letter to the Romans, the Apostle Paul alluded to the Holy Spirit as "the Spirit of Holiness" (Rom. 1:4). When a person is Born Again, the spiritual transaction that takes place is that that person's heart is actually "regenerated," which is to say that his/her human spirit is brought back to life from languishing in spiritual death (see Eph. 2:1). What effects this miraculous transaction is the infusion of the Life of God, the Divine Nature, into the human spirit.

Thus, at the rebirth, we are, as we say, "filled with the Spirit." The Spirit with which we are filled is the *Holy* Spirit, or the "Spirit of Holiness." In other words, when we are born again, our Spirit is impregnated with "the Spirit of Holiness." The indwelling of the Spirit of Holiness within our hearts enables us to manifest the holiness of the Divine Nature in our outward "behavior," as Peter indicated. Albeit, because the carnal nature is not eradicated, or removed, but co-exists contemporaneously within us as well, we are not able to express or live out the holiness of God with the same absolute perfection as it exists in the Divine Nature. Nevertheless, the more we "walk by the Spirit," the less we "carry out the desires of the flesh" (Gal. 5:16).

Conversely, those who have not been regenerated by the infusion of the Holy Spirit cannot possibly live truly holy. Some people may live relatively "good" lives, but "good" is not "holy." Only God is truly *Holy*. Without holiness, "no man will see the Lord" (Heb. 12:14). Multitudes of people live relatively "good" lives, compared to the multitudes of overtly *evil* people who have lived or are now living. But, *good* is not the same as *holy*. Only God is truly *Holy*.

Contrary to the thanksgiving prose recited by so many before meals, God is more than just "good" and "great," God is *Holy*! If you want to have Eternal fellowship with God, you must be filled with holiness, not just be "good."

The Apostle Peter, speaking words inspired by the Holy Spirit, declared the Church consists not of people who are merely *good*, but of people who are **Holy** — "a **Holy** nation":

> But you are a chosen race, a royal priesthood, a **Holy** nation, a people for God's own possession, that you may proclaim the excellencies of Him who has called you out of darkness into His marvelous light....Beloved, I urge you as aliens and strangers to abstain from fleshly lusts, which wage war against the soul. Keep your behavior excellent among the Gentiles, so that in the thing in which they slander you as evildoers, they may on account of your good deeds, as they observe them, glorify God in the day of visitation. (1 Pet. 2:9-12)

Make no mistake about it, repentance and sanctification are both vital and essential elements of true salvation, and mandatory requisites for attaining unto Eternal Life. To believe in Jesus Christ is to believe the Word of God, all of it, for He is the personification of the Word (Jn. 1:1). To believe in Jesus Christ is to receive Him, to receive Him is to obey Him. To obey Jesus Christ is to obey His written Word, the Bible. Obedience is the ultimate objective of repentance and the sanctification of the Spirit.

Anyone who does not obey Jesus Christ through obeying God's Word through a purified heart and sanctified conduct, simply does not know God, and has not entered into communion and fellowship with Him. And, anyone who says he does know God, but does not obey His commandments and live a holy life, God Himself calls an outright "liar":

> And by this we know that we have come to know Him, if we keep His commandments. The one who says, "I have come to know Him," and does not keep His commandments, is a liar, and the truth is not in him; but whoever keeps His word, in him the love of God has truly been perfected. By this we know that we are in Him: the one who says he abides in Him ought himself to walk in the same manner as He walked. (1 Jn. 2:3-6)

Anyone who does not obey God's commandments does not know God, and he certainly does not love God either, as John says in the above passage. He says it is the person who obeys God's commandments in whom "the love of God has truly been perfected." And, John received that information on good authority too, from none other than Jesus Himself, who he himself heard say:

> If you love Me, you will keep My commandments. (Jn. 14:15)

> He who has My commandments and keeps them, he it is who loves Me; and he who loves me shall be loved by My Father, and I will love him, and will disclose Myself to him. (Jn. 14:21)

Jesus answered and said to him, "If anyone loves Me, he will keep My word; and My Father will love him, and We will come to him, and make Our abode with him. He who does not love Me does not keep My words; and the word which you hear is not Mine, but the Father's who sent Me!" (Jn. 14:23,24)

If you keep My commandments, you will abide in My love; just as I have kept My Father's commandments, and abide in His love. (Jn. 15:10)

To summarize, the point that is being established here is that repentance and the process of sanctification which ensues are absolutely vital to the spiritual livelihood of every believer.

The problem with this second category of hearers, those with "rocky ground," is that their repentance is not deep enough. They are only willing to repent of "surface" and external sins, and not the sinful attitudes that lie deep within their hearts. Until they repent of that deeper sinfulness and carnality, the sanctification process can only be incomplete, which will eventually prove to be spiritually fatal, as the parable goes on to indicate, in that these hearers ultimately fell away from faith in and their relationship with Jesus.

Chapter Seven

Temporary Believers

Jesus' narrative concerning this second category of hearers, those who are like "rocky ground," goes on to reveal that these people are only "*temporary* believers." Jesus said of them: "and they have no firm root in themselves, but are only temporary" (Mk. 4:17). Luke's account of this part of Jesus' parable aptly describes their walk this way: "they believe for a while, and in time of temptation fall away" (Lk. 8:13). This is an extremely crucial statement in that Jesus Himself explicitly and definitively indicates that these people were indeed bona fide "believers" rather than bogus believers as the proponents of the "once saved always saved" Eternal Security doctrine allege. Jesus said, "they believe for a while," and to contend otherwise is to call Jesus a liar. Likewise, to say they did not subsequently fall away after having truly believed is to call Jesus a liar as well, for Jesus explicitly stated, "and in time of temptation (they) fall away."

Unfortunately, there are many people today who are of this category of only *temporary* believers. There was a point at which they truly believed in and accepted the Gospel of Christ, and were thereby saved. At first, they are willing to follow Jesus and obey His Word. But, later, when they begin to meet with some temptation (Lk. 8:13), and afflictions and persecutions (Mk. 4:17), these temporary believers fall away.

We will discuss the stumbling-stones over which this category of hearers stumble and which cause them to fall away, as well as the matter of falling away itself in the next two chapters. In this chapter, however, we just want to focus on the fact that these people are indeed temporary believers.

Paying the Price

One thing for which this ilk of hearers can be commended is that at least their initial response to the Gospel was the right and rational response. They apparently realized they were lost and eternally undone without the salvation of the Savior, and they even acknowledged that Jesus was the only true Savior. They were at least rational enough not to want to remain lost, but rather they wanted to be saved. Those of this category of hearers are not so foolish as to overtly choose, by rejecting the Savior, eternal banishment to the unquenchable flames of a real Hell, though it may be, however, that they did primarily view Jesus as their "fire escape" from Hell.

Sadly, it may be that of all those who respond to the Gospel there are more of this category of temporary believers than any other. They will respond to an altar call, walk the aisle and shake the preacher's hand, publicly acknowledge they are a sinner, and dutifully repeat a "sinner's prayer," if that is what they must do, to salve their conscience and escape eternal damnation. They are willing to do all that, if they must. But, the truth of the matter, as time alone will tell, is that they want to be a recipient of all the benefits of the program, but they aren't really ready, prepared, or willing to pay the premiums.

Now, frankly, this is not the exclusive fault of these respondents. I must regretfully and chagrinfully admit as a preacher myself that many "convert candidates" have been misled by some of my preacher colleagues into believing that this whole matter of salvation and committing your life to Jesus "will not cost you anything." Now I know what those who make such ill-advised statements are meaning to say, which is that there is nothing we can do to *earn* salvation and rightstanding with God, and that Jesus Himself paid the only price by which our redemption could be purchased, which was His own shed blood. That certainly is true. But, to simply say that committing your life to Jesus "will not cost you anything," though it may sound good and appealing, is a very unfortunate and actually incorrect choice of verbiage. It is no wonder people will respond affirmatively to an invitation such as that. You really can't blame them.

However, the real truth is that to become a child of God through surrendering your life to Jesus will cost you *everything*. A true believer who earnestly and fervently serves and obeys the Lord with all his heart will eventually have surrendered all he is and has to the Lord. Jesus said a person must be willing to completely "lose" his own life for the sake of finding Jesus' Life, which is the Eternal Life (Mat. 10:39; 1 Jn. 1:1,2). That sounds to me like it will cost a person *everything* to be a true follower of Jesus Christ. Make no mistake about it, my friend, entering into Eternal Life requires an eventual complete surrender of *everything* we are and have unto God, by Whom we were originally created and from Whose Being we originally emanated.

The Gospel is full of paradoxes. One of the foremost and essential paradoxes of the Kingdom of God is that in order to live, you must die. The Apostle Paul said that true believers are "always carrying about in the body the *dying* of Jesus that the *life* of Jesus also may be manifested in our body" (2 Cor. 4:10, italics added by author). "The dying of Jesus" is death to every form of sin and self. In order for any true believer to manifest in his own life the pure Life of Jesus, he or she must undergo the same process of death to self Jesus did during His fleshly manifestation on Earth, which is what Paul was referring to by the term "the dying of Jesus":

> "For we who live are constantly being delivered over to death for Jesus' sake, that the life of Jesus also may be manifested in our mortal flesh. So death works in us...." (2 Cor. 4:11,12)

Counting the Cost

Will it cost you something to serve Jesus?

You better believe it will. You must surrender your entire being — spirit, soul, and body — over to Jesus. You must die to every form of sin and unrighteousness (Rom. 6:1-11). You must put to death the sinful deeds of the fleshly body (Gal. 5:24). And, you must submit your mind, will, and emotions to the Lordship of Jesus Christ.

Jesus in no way preached an "easy gospel," as some allege today. He never used euphemistic persuasion to call people to Himself. He never expected people to come to Him unadvisedly. Quite to the contrary, He taught that people should first *"count the cost"* before they make a decision to follow after Him, because every true disciple, then and now, is required to carry his own personal cross of affliction and persecution:

> Now great multitudes were going along with Him; and He turned and said to them, "If anyone comes to Me, and does not hate (footnote: i.e., by comparison of his love for Me) his own father and mother and wife and children and brothers and sisters, yes, and even his own life, he cannot be My disciple. Whoever does not carry his own cross and come after Me cannot be My disciple. For which one of you, when he wants to build a tower, does not first sit down and calculate (count) the cost, to see if he has enough to complete it?" (Lk. 14:28)

Nothing could be more apropos in the case of these hearers of the Word who Jesus said are like "rocky ground." They did not first sit down and calculate the cost of discipleship, and realistically calculate what following Jesus was going to cost them. They did not foresee that there was going to be crosses to bear, that they were going to have to endure against many tribulations, temptations, tests, and trials. So, "in time of temptation (they) fall away," Luke's synopsis quotes Jesus as saying. Mark's account says, "when affliction or persecution arises because of the word, immediately they fall away" (Mk. 4:17).

These people indeed are only *temporary* believers. They are willing to respond affirmatively to the Gospel in order to be saved and to escape Hell. But, they are not willing to effect a complete surrender and repentance. Nor are they willing to die totally to self and sin, and relinquish lordship over their own lives. Some are willing to effect a superficial repentance of surface sins, but not a complete repentance of the evil motivations which pervade the unredeemed soul. Much less are they willing to offensively resist the enemy on the battlefield of temptation, affliction, and persecution, in order to follow after Jesus.

Temporary believers, unfortunately, are only willing to stay married to Jesus and live the Christian life as long as life is easy and convenient and doesn't cost them anything, as long as life is full of nothing but "showers of blessings." But, when the showers of blessings start to become mixed with intermittent droughts of even only relatively minor affliction and persecution, that is, when the sun arises, as Jesus put it in the parable, and "the heat is on," and their commitment is tested a little, *temporary* believers immediately want to dissolve the relationship, with a quick and easy, no-muss, no-fuss, no-fault divorce after the manner of the divorces meted out by our courts today.

But, that is not the way it is with *true* believers. True believers are in this thing *forever*. When they make their commitment to Jesus, they do it knowing full well it is *Eternal Life*, an everlasting life of never-ending fellowship with God, they've bought into, and they are eternally committed to Him through thick and thin, and no matter what may come, hell or high water. Indeed, if you have the great honor and privilege of living for Jesus in this world before being united with Him in the Spirit, it is guaranteed you will indeed experience both — hell and high water. True believers forsake all else in order to obtain the "costly pearl" (Mat. 13:45,46) of *Eternal* Life, and *Eternal* Life is what they will indeed be rewarded with in the end.

Indeed, this commitment to follow after Jesus has been known to cost some people literally everything. The Apostle Peter, after less than three years of following after Jesus, speaking apparently on behalf of the Twelve Apostles of the Lamb, railed at Jesus, "Behold, we have left everything and followed You" (Mk. 10:28). Overlooking Peter's obvious rancor, Jesus in essence replied that such may indeed be the cost for earnest followers:

> And He said to them, "Truly I say to you, there is no one who has left house or wife or brothers or parents or children, for the sake of the kingdom of God, who shall not receive many times as much at this time and in the age to come, Eternal Life." (Lk. 18:29,30)

Indeed, there has been more than one resolute believer down through the ages who has had to give up houses, wives, brothers, parents, children, friends, colleagues, business and vocational pursuits, and the like, in order to follow after Jesus and the revealed Will of God. It is terribly unfortunate and painful, but sometimes friends, relatives, and loved ones simply refuse to follow along with you when you make the decision to follow Jesus. Nevertheless, Jesus said anyone who is not willing to bear that cross of persecution and to follow after Him, is not worthy of Him. There is a chorus we sing that talks about all this, which says:

> I have decided to follow Jesus.
> I have decided to follow Jesus.
> I have decided to follow Jesus.
> No turning back, no turning back.
>
> Though none go with me, yet I will follow.
> Though none go with me, yet I will follow.
> Though none go with me, yet I will follow.
> No turning back, No turning back.

I have personally known people who have had to quite literally "give up" friends and loved ones, in order to follow Jesus; some for only a while, some forever. It didn't *have* to be that way, and the believer certainly did not *want* it to be that way, but that is the way it happened nonetheless, because those friends and loved ones simply refused to accompany them on the path they had chosen to follow, the path of Eternal Life and fellowship with God.

I have personal knowledge of men called to the ministry who had no choice but to "give up" loved ones, in order to follow and obey Jesus and His revealed Will for their lives, and in order to pursue the call of God upon them. There were certain ministers of the past who were greatly used of God who experienced such heart-rending dilemmas with regard to family members, who, as they went on to be faithful to God, received an eternal, unfathomable reward that made it all worth it. So also are there contemporary ministers with a great call upon their life who shall be likewise rewarded for their undeterred faithfulness.

We must be willing to follow Jesus no matter what the cost. Otherwise, we will not be worthy of Him (Mat. 10:37,38). In fact, Jesus once even went so far as to declare, "No one of you can be My disciple who does not give up all his own possessions" (Lk. 14:33). Spiritually speaking, every *true* saint of God does indeed eventually "give up" everything he is and has; that is to say, he or she surrenders any claim of personal ownership and lordship of everything unto the Lord.

But, praise God, God is not a *"taker,"* despite the wholly erroneous statement of Job: "The Lord gave and the Lord hath taken away" (Job 1:21), which misstatement he later retracted in dust and ashes, and utter shame and chagrin (42:1-6). Rather, God is only a *Giver*. "God so loved the world that He gave..." (Jn. 3:16). God gave even His only begotten Son, because He is a Giver by Nature. He gives because He cannot help Himself. As someone has so aptly said, "You can give without loving, but you cannot love without giving."

And so, God, who IS Love and from whom Agape-Love emanates (1 Jn. 4:7,8), is absolutely compelled by His overwhelming Love-Nature to give. He has absolutely no desire or interest in taking things away from people He has bestowed to them, especially not because of any need of His own. How ludicrous and even blasphemous the notion! That would make Him a selfish thief, which He is not. Satan is the thief, who steals, kills, and destroys (Jn. 10:10). Besides, God doesn't need anything we have:

> The God who made the world and all things in it, since He is Lord of heaven and earth, does not dwell in temples made with hands; neither is He served by human hands, as though he needed anything, since He Himself gives... (Acts 17:24,25)

No, God is not a taker, but a Giver. It's just that He insists on being Lord over everything, as He indeed is. He requires that we abdicate lordship and rights of ownership of everything we have and are, and give it to Him, in order that Jesus may indeed be Lord of All that pertains to us. And, praise God when we do relinquish the "things" pertaining to this world in order to seek first His Kingdom and His righteousness, He actually returns all those "things" we need for life, because He well knows that we need all these "things" (Mat. 6:32,33).

Moreover, He even returns them to us in multiplied measure, "a hundred times as much," and not "when we all get to Heaven," or "in the sweet by and by," but in the sweet here and "now in the present age" (Mk. 10:30). For you see, we won't need those things in Heaven; we only need them now in this life here on planet Earth.

Indeed, there is a cost for discipleship, but true believers are willing to pay the price, whatever it may be. Temporary believers, however, are not. When things begin to get difficult, and they meet with a little trouble, tribulation, and hardship, temporary believers start to wither.

The Tell-tale Sign

At first, it may be somewhat difficult to tell if a person is going to eventually prove to be only a temporary believer. In fact, the ones who do prove to be only temporary, may seem to be least likely to ever fall away from the faith and following after Jesus. Curiously, Jesus indicated that the tip-off, or the "tell-tale sign" that they are of this category of temporary believers is their initial reaction to the Gospel when they first accept it, which is that they "immediately receive it with joy" (Mk. 4:16). In other words, their immediate response is one of great exuberance and enthusiasm, and they seem ecstatic about becoming a Christian.

Now, the problem is: who would want to find fault with that? And, certainly, anyone who did would most likely be considered by others to be some sort of religious "Scrooge," bah-humbugging someone's rightful excitement over having been saved.

As strange and paradoxical as it may seem, however, Jesus is in fact indicating here in this portion of the parable that this initial reaction of exuberance is itself the "tell-tale sign" that these "rocky grounders" are only temporary believers. Now, I realize this seems enigmatic and difficult to understand with the carnal mind, but it is, nevertheless, what Jesus is saying here.

Albeit, by no means is this to say that there is not, or should not be, a certain amount of sincere jubilation when a person gives his life to Jesus. Without question, it is the greatest thing that will ever happen to any person, and there is great cause and justification for rejoicing. Indeed, the Bible says that even the angels rejoice in Heaven whenever a sinner repents. Other believers are certainly justified in rejoicing and giving thanks as well.

Nevertheless, it is also true that when a person is first being confronted with the Truth of the Gospel, and the Holy Spirit is drawing him to Jesus, he is at that moment being convinced and convicted of his utter sinfulness and spiritual poverty. In this valley of decision, the Word of God becomes a mirror of the soul, effecting some sober and sorrowful reflection with regard to one's own wretchedness against the Image of a Holy and Righteous God. This is how the Holy Spirit brings people to the repentance that leads to salvation. For, the first and foremost step to salvation is one's realization that he is indeed a lost and undone sinner, and that he desperately needs the saving of the Savior.

When confronted with these harsh realizations, most people are not leaping very high in jubilant exultation. Quite on the contrary, at this point, more often than not, when a person is having a genuine encounter with God and genuinely being wooed by the Holy Spirit to Jesus, that person soon begins to experience a very sobering "godly sorrow," a "sorrow that is according to the will of God," which "produces a repentance without regret, leading to salvation" (2 Cor. 7:10). As this is occurring, there is usually more weeping than rejoicing, of tears of sorrow, repentance, and even mourning, which is all in accordance with Scripture:

> Draw near to God and He will draw near to you. Cleanse your hands, you sinners; and purify your hearts, you double-minded. Be miserable and mourn and weep; let your laughter be turned into mourning, and your joy to gloom. (Jas. 4:8,9)

But, oh how cleansing are those tears! All uncleanness is washed away in the tide of those tears of repentance, until that person can exclaim, "Clean! Clean! Clean before my Lord!" Then, in the passage of time, those tears of sorrow progressively are converted to tears of joy, as the new believer begins to realize that he is forgiven, pardoned, justified, redeemed, and has begun the process of being conformed into the Image of Christ (Rom. 8:29). Nonetheless, in the case of those who have made a complete surrender of their lives unto Jesus and have been thoroughly transformed, the "godly sorrow" precedes the joy.

In the case of these temporary believers, however, it did not happen that way. Rather, Jesus said, "When they hear the word, immediately receive it with joy" (Mk. 4:16). Godly sorrow did not precede their joy, but instead their joy came "immediately." Apparently, according to what Jesus said, these "rocky grounders" did not have any godly sorrow, producing repentance, leading to salvation (2 Cor. 7:10). As already discussed previously, their repentance was very, very shallow. Hence, because they still had a bedrock of sin lying beneath their top-soil of superficial repentance, their roots were not able to grow sufficiently deep into Jesus to sustain them when trials and tribulations came their way. Thus, because they did not have an adequate root system, when the sun arose with its torrid rays of trials, afflictions, and persecutions, they were scorched, and ultimately withered away.

In the next chapter we examine the "afflictions and persecutions," which when they came, according to what Jesus said, caused these temporary believers to fall away.

Chapter Eight

Affliction and Persecution

Mark 4:6,17
6 And after the sun had risen, it was scorched; and because it had no root, it withered away.
17 and they have no firm root in themselves, but are only temporary; then, when affliction and persecution arises because of the word, immediately they fall away.

Nowhere has God promised believers a rose garden. Some people have a confused understanding of what Jesus meant when He said, "I came that they might have life, and might have it abundantly" (Jn. 10:10).

The Greek word translated "life" is not a reference to physical existence on Earth, per se. That word "zoe," is actually the word God uses in Scripture for spiritual life; that is, the Eternal Life. Jesus did come to bring us that Life in overflowing abundance. In the same regard, the Apostle Peter even said, "His divine power has granted to us everything pertaining to life (zoe) and godliness" (2 Pet. 1:3).

The Abundant Life Jesus came to give every true believer is the Eternal Life, His Life, which indwells every true, Born Again (there is no other kind) believer in the person of the Holy Spirit. God spares nothing in giving believers that Life. He pours His Life into us in abounding superfluity, which is what the Greek word Jesus used that is translated "abundantly" means. It means that Jesus came to give us His Life in overflowing measure. It means we have exceedingly more than we will ever need to utilize in any circumstance.

That is the Abundant Life Jesus was talking about. He was not referring to our span of physical existence in this present world. He was not saying that our existence in this world would be so "abundant" so as to be absolutely free of any negative or adverse circumstances. No, such a euphoric state of utopia will never exist on planet Earth in the present age.

Much to the contrary, Jesus forthrightly declared, "In this world you will have tribulation" (Jn. 16:33). The Apostle Paul said, "Through

MANY tribulations we must enter the kingdom of God" (Acts 14:22). Life in this present world is full of tribulations.

The Abundant Life of Jesus is abundant with nothing but "goodness and righteousness and truth" (Eph. 5:39). Nevertheless, our physical existence in this present world is inevitably abundant with "the sufferings of Christ": "The sufferings of Christ are ours in abundance" (2 Cor. 1:5). Especially in these last days in which we live are our lives full of tribulations and difficulties, something which the Spirit of God predicted: "But realize this, that in the last days difficult times will come" (2 Tim. 3:1).

Now all these admonitions concerning tribulation are directed to believers. Believers are not impervious to tribulations. No one who lives in this present world on planet Earth is impervious to tribulation. It comes with the territory, as they say. In fact, the real truth is that believers may be the target of more adversity than unbelievers. It's just that believers have the wherewithal to overcome every adversity. This was the essence of what the Apostle Paul wrote to the young minister Timothy, who had learned greatly under the tutelage of Paul, not only from his extraordinary revelation knowledge, but also from his exemplary life, which was replete with afflictions and persecutions:

> But you followed my teaching, conduct, purpose, faith, patience, love, perseverance, persecutions and sufferings, such as happened to me at Antioch, at Iconium and at Lystra; what persecutions I endured, and out of them all the Lord delivered me! And indeed, all who desire to live godly in Christ Jesus will be persecuted. (2 Tim. 3:10-12)

Under the inspiration of the Holy Spirit, Paul declared that *everyone* who sincerely desires to live godly in Christ Jesus in this world will indeed be persecuted. Believers, the Born Again children of God, are the only ones who are "in Christ Jesus." Paul said all believers "who desire to live godly" will be persecuted. He didn't say they "*might be.*" He said they "will be" persecuted. It is not even required that a believer be entirely perfected in godly living in order to be persecuted, necessarily, but just have the "desire" to live godly in Christ Jesus.

The more conformed into the Image of Jesus (Rom. 8:29) and less conformed to the world (Rom. 12:2) a believer becomes, the more persecution he will experience in this world through those who are not conformed into His Image, who walk "according to the course of this world, according to the prince of the power of the air" (Eph. 2:2).

"Yes, but we should not 'believe' for persecution," some say today, "because if we do, then we will be sure to get it."

My friend, my Bible says if you desire to live godly in Christ Jesus, you "**will be** persecuted," whether you are "believing" for it or not. Jesus foretold His death, burial, and resurrection many times. He told the apostles that He would be mocked, spit upon, and beaten. Were all those things fulfilled because He made a "bad confession" and was "believing" for it? Jesus forewarned the apostles they would be mistreated, persecuted, and even killed for the sake of the Gospel. Were those things, including the eventual martyrdom of those great men, fulfilled because they were "believing" for it? Did the great Apostle Paul experience all the afflictions and persecutions he experienced, which he enumerates seemingly endlessly in Second Corinthians 11:23-28, because he was "believing" for them? How absurd!

It is when someone who purports to be a believer is *not* being persecuted and afflicted with adversity that I begin to seriously wonder why not! God's Word says, "**all** who desire to live godly in Christ Jesus **will be** persecuted." I say let God be true and every man a liar. Anyone who is not being persecuted to some degree, had better do some checking to see how he is doing in the godly living department.

What is Affliction and Persecution?

Generally speaking, the term "affliction" in the Bible connotes adverse circumstances or conditions, such as, trouble, trial, difficulty, grief, hardship, anxiety, and the like. Bodily and mental sickness, disease, and pain are also forms of affliction. These physical afflictions, however, were borne by Jesus Christ on the cross at Calvary, and by His stripes we were healed (Is. 53). Nevertheless, those who have not yet received that revelation, continue to be afflicted. Even knowledgeable believers, though, are not impervious to the enemy's attempts to afflict physically, only they must offensively resist him, and refuse to passively accept and receive infirmities Jesus "took" (*vicariously bore*) and diseases Jesus "carried away" (*removed*) at Calvary (Mat. 8:17, italics added by author).

"Persecution," on the other hand, usually refers to adversity brought against a person or group of persons by another person or group of persons. Persecution can range from subtle contrariety to repression to oppression to physical harm and abuse, and all the way to outright murder.

Affliction and persecution would also be included in what the Bible terms "tribulation." We have already seen several Scriptures concerning the fact that our lives in this world will be intrinsically laden with tribulations. Most of us, however may not be able to readily identify with the term "tribulations," until it is rendered as its literal meaning — "pressures."

Most people can readily identify with having "pressures" in their lives. Understanding that "tribulation" is "pressure" makes it easier to understand what Jesus meant when He said that "in this world" we would have "tribulations." He meant that during the course of our lives we would often experience a variety of "pressures." Nearly every day of our lives, especially in this hectic, fast-paced modern era, we are inundated with pressures of various types and degrees, just as Jesus predicted.

Who Authors Affliction and Persecution?

Contrary to many religious ideologies, the Word of God attributes authorship of all adversity to the "adversary," Satan: "Your adversary, the devil, prowls about like a roaring lion, seeking someone to devour" (1 Pet. 5:8). It is totally unScriptural to purport, however, that God cannot, has not, or does not inflict various forms and degrees of temporal judgments and disciplinary actions on individuals, groups, and even whole nations. God can, has, and does anything He pleases in agreement with His Word. He is Sovereign. Nevertheless, pure adversity is only attributable to Satan.

Satan is the adversary of everyone, but especially of believers. He hates God and His entire Creation, especially "the apple of His eye" — His redeemed children. Now Satan cannot harm God in any way, so he has mounted a vicious, never-relenting battle against all of God's Creation, and especially against his arch-nemesis, the Church.

When Adam committed high treason against God in the Garden of Eden, he handed over to Satan the dominion and surrogate lordship of this world which God had delegated unto the Sons of Men (Adam's progeny) [Ps. 115:16]. Thereby, Satan became "the god of this world" (2 Cor. 4:4), "the ruler of the world" (Jn. 14:30). By virtue of Man's fall into perdition, Satan now had rulership over the elements and order of this world. The entire Creation became enslaved to the effects of his unrighteous nature corruption (Rom. 8:21). From that moment on, the entire creation eagerly awaited the manifestation of the redeemed Sons of God, true believers, who would resist, oppose, and arrest Satan and his adverse works through the authority given them "over all the power of the enemy" (Lk. 10:19) by the Lord Jesus Christ.

Satan has the power in the present age to inflict adversity upon those who do not resist him. He never ceases in his evil and adverse works, some of which are to: steal, kill, destroy, deceive, harass, hinder, depress, oppress, possess, tempt, accuse, pervert, blind, captivate, torment, confuse, condemn, provoke, afflict, corrupt, and persecute.

But, praise God, the very purpose of Jesus Christ's appearance was: "that He might destroy the works of the devil" (1 Jn. 3:9). And, He *has* destroyed the works of the devil, but it is up to the redeemed to execute that destruction, at least in their own personal regard, through the authority Jesus has delegated to them.

Satan is the adversary, who is *against* us, but God is **FOR** us. David said, "This I know, that God is for me" (Ps. 56:9). If he didn't know anything else, he knew one thing — that his God was *for* him, and **not** *against* him. If a believer does not know anything else, he needs to know one thing for sure — God is *for* him, and **not** *against* him.

Satan authors adversity, but God authors good! God is forever trying to bring good into our lives. The Bible says, "every good thing bestowed and every perfect gift is from above, coming down from the Father of Lights" (Jas. 1:17). In the verse preceding that verse, God specifically warns us not to be deceived concerning that fact. Yet, so many people *are* deceived because they have bought the devil's lie that God is the one who is bringing all the bad into people's lives. But that is only a vicious lie, under which he camouflages himself and his own destructive works.

So many people are blaming God for the terrible things the devil has been doing all along. They have been duped into believing God has been bringing all the adversity and difficulties into their lives. They begin to blame God.

Yet, the Bible tells us explicitly that when we are experiencing a temptation, test, or trial, we should not say, "'I am being tempted by God'; for God cannot be tempted by evil, and He Himself does not tempt anyone" (Jas. 1:13). It is not God who is bringing evil and adversity into our lives. As Job was admonished by Elihu, "Far be it from God to do wickedness, and from the Almighty do wrong....Surely God will not act wickedly, and the Almighty will not pervert justice" (Job 34:10-12).

"God is light, and in Him there is no darkness at all"(1 Jn. 1:5), which means there is absolutely no evil in God. Therefore, it would be impossible for Him to use evil toward us. Since, as James said, "God cannot be tempted by evil," it would be a gross perversion of His Divine Righteousness for Him to bring such things upon anyone else, but rather, as the passage explicitly says, "He Himself does not tempt anyone."

Why Do Affliction and Persecution Come?

Besides the reasons already discussed, Jesus said the reason affliction and persecutions come is "because of the word" (Mk. 4:17). It is no coincidence that while the Word is being sown into the hearts of these hearers, Satan is bringing external affliction and persecutions into their lives.

Contrary to the pious-sounding preaching of some people, God in no wise intends for believers to be foolishly ignorant of the schemes of the devil. That would only give the enemy an overwhelming advantage. God explicitly warns against that: "in order that no advantage be taken of us by Satan; for we are not ignorant of his schemes" (2 Cor. 2:11). The word translated "schemes" here, and in the passage, "Put on the full armor of God, that you may be able to stand firm against the schemes of the devil" (Eph. 6:11), actually connotes "strategic battle plans" in the original language. It speaks of military generals gathered around a battlefield map, carefully plotting out strategic battle plans.

This is precisely what the Holy Spirit is revealing about our enemy, the devil — that he carefully contrives strategic battle plans to launch against believers. His tactics are well conceived, and are by no means happenstance. He has a strategic battle plan tailor-made for each individual believer. He looks for chinks in the believer's armor, which is precisely the reason it is so essential that every believer "put on the full armor of God, that you may be able to stand firm against the schemes of the devil."

Any battle-wise, battle-tested soldier will tell you that the most stupid and potentially fatal mistake a soldier can make is to not be apprised concerning the "modus operandi" of the enemy. If you are informed concerning the enemy's usual methods, then you have a distinct advantage over him, rather than vice-versa. One of the most vital and extensive parts of a soldier's pre-battle training is instruction on the means and methods of the enemy; in other words — his strategic battle plans. Anyone who does not give attention to that block of instruction is not only stupid, but more often than not will not survive the battle. Likewise, it is stupid and oftentimes deadly for a believer not to be apprised concerning the strategic battle plans of his adversary, the devil. That only gives him a decided and unnecessary advantage. God does not intend for believers to be uninformed or ignorant concerning Satan's schemes and devices. Rather, He wants us to be informed concerning them, in order that we "may be able to stand firm against" them.

The next most essential element of a soldier's battle training is instruction on his own weapon. He must become thoroughly familiarized with every aspect of proper usage and maintenance of that weapon. His survival depends on it. He must learn how to become a skilled marksman with his weapon, and how to insure that it continuously remains in proper working order.

Similarly, believers are in an all-out, life or death, battle. It is a *spiritual* battle, fought in the *spiritual* realm, against *spiritual* foes (Eph. 6:12). Thus, we must use *spiritual* weapons, for fleshly weapons are utterly useless and powerless in this *spiritual* battle: "For the weapons of our warfare are not of the flesh, but divinely powerful for the destruction of fortresses" (2 Cor. 10:4).

The chief offensive weapon in the believer's arsenal is "the word of the Spirit, which is the word of God" (Eph. 6:17). The Word of God can be used to successfully resist the enemy every time. The spiritual foes against whom we battle are utterly defeated on every battle front when the all-powerful Sword of God's Spirit is wielded. Every believer must become thoroughly acquainted with his weapon, and through continuous practice become a skilled marksman with it. "All Scripture" is the believer's weapon, with which he is more than adequately equipped for defeat of every foe (2 Tim. 3:16,17).

You see, the fulness of God's power is contained in His Word! Every Word God has ever spoken is "the word of His power" (Heb. 1:3). That means that all of God's omnipotence is released and executed by His spoken (Rhema) Word, which is the exact means by which He created the entire Creation, according to Moses' account. Jesus Himself is the Creator (Col. 1:16), and the Word of God Embodied (Jn. 1:10), and thus He Himself is "the power of God" (1 Cor. 1:24). When God's Word is spoken in accordance with His Ways to effect His Will, all the same might that conquered death and created the entire Creation is unleashed.

Moreover, in cases of inspired application, God's Word will accomplish yet today all it has ever accomplished as it is spoken by a believer into the atmosphere of the Creation. God says He personally watches over His Word to execute it (Jer. 1:12). He promises it will accomplish exactly what it says: "It shall not return to Me empty, without accomplishing what I desire, and without succeeding in the matter for which I sent it" (Is. 55:11).

Now Satan knows the truth of all this more than most people, including most believers. He is quite aware of the omnipotent might of God's Word. And, he knows that all of God's omnipotence is unleashed through His Word. He is experientially cognizant that God's Word has more than ample might to "destroy the works of the devil" (1 Jn. 3:8). He knows the destruction wreaked against his evil works through the discharge of the "weapons of our warfare."

Satan has experienced firsthand the awesome power unleashed against him by "doers of the Word." He knows the validity of Jesus' Words: "Behold, I have given you authority to tread upon serpents and scorpions, and over all the power of the enemy, and nothing shall injure you" (Lk. 10:19). He knows that he will have to flee in terror from the believer who is submitted to God and who offensively, proactively resists the devil with the spiritual weapons of spiritual warfare. He knows the believer who puts on the whole armor of God and boldly wields the Sword of the Spirit cannot be overcome by the greatest of his strategic battle plans.

So, it is because of all these truths concerning God's Word that Satan brings affliction and persecution against believers — "because of the word" — "the word of His power." Inundating with a barrage of affliction and persecution is his strategic battle plan against especially new as well as immature believers, in an attempt to steal the Word from their heart before it can take root and begin to produce some fruit.

Jesus said people are like rocky ground, "when affliction and persecution arises because of the word, immediately they fall away" (Mk. 4:17). That is the ultimate goal Satan is aiming for — to cause everyone who has made a commitment to serve the Lord to fall away. In order to do that, he attempts to get the new and spiritually undeveloped believers to doubt the validity of the Word of God, and the ability of God to perform it in their own lives by inundating them with a flood of affliction and persecution. Then, as they become doubtful, discouraged, and disheartened, their faith in the Word begins to wane, and they cease to boldly utilize their arsenal of spiritual weapons. They also fail to put on the whole armor of God to defend themselves against the attack of the enemy.

Eventually, the believer who has ceased to offensively and defensively resist the enemy will be overcome by his strategic battle plans. Or, as Jesus said it, they will soon "fall away." This is the plight of this category of hearers — when afflictions and persecutions come into their lives because of the Word, they fall away, because they are only temporary believers.

This matter of whether or not a believer can fall away has been a topic of great controversy and debate in many factions of the Church. To be sure, it is a subject that many ministers avoid and evade whenever possible. However, it is virtually impossible to avoid this issue when expounding upon the Parable of the Sower. Moreover, it would be absolutely unconscionable to omit this topic from a dissertation concerning "the mystery of the Kingdom" of God, to which it is central and essential. Thus, I have devoted the next chapter entirely to this very important issue of believers falling away as Jesus said these "rocky grounders" did.

Chapter Nine

Falling Away

Jesus specifically said that in the case of this second category of hearers: "when affliction and persecution arises because of the word, immediately they fall away" (Mk. 4:17). According to Jesus, the result when they met with adversity after having believed is that "immediately they fall away." According to the doctrine of a number of Christian denominations today, this just cannot be so. Nevertheless, according to Jesus and God's Word, it is immutably so.

Before going any further, some readers may note that the King James Version says they were "offended," rather than that they fell away. However, this Elizabethan English usage does not accurately convey the intention of the original language. In the Greek, that word actually means to cause someone to stumble with the end result of falling. It is always used metaphorically to connote a falling away. Most translations other than the King James Version do indicate a falling away in this passage and others where the same Greek word is used.

There are a number of Christian denominations today who espouse what is commonly known as "the doctrine of eternal security." Simply stated, this belief purports that once a person has made a verbal confession of Jesus Christ as his Savior, there is virtually no way he can ever lose his salvation or fall away, but that somehow, someway, God guarantees his eventual salvation; hence, that person's salvation is "eternally secure."

While I must say such an ideology would be extremely convenient, it is nonetheless quite unScriptural. Many people have used the auspices of this doctrine for license to continue in their sin and licentiousness under this false sense of "eternal security," by which they are duped into believing they shall escape divine judgment for their deeds.

Now this is not at all to say that salvation for true, obedient believers is not eternally secure. On the contrary, the salvation and redemption that Jesus purchased with His own blood is most sure and forever secure. The obedient believer can be utterly assured of his salvation, and know with total certainty that he has Eternal Life: "These things I have written to you who believe in the name of the Son of God, in order that you may know that you have eternal life" (1 Jn. 5:13).

God certainly does not want any believer to be in a quandary concerning his salvation and eternal destiny. Yet, at the same time, He has published innumerable warnings and exhortations in His Word concerning the fact that it is quite possible for someone who confesses Jesus Christ as Lord and Savior to fall away from following Him and consequently lose his salvation.

Scriptures regarding believers falling away of which I have personal knowledge number at nearly one-hundred. Space simply will not permit an exhaustive study of them all, but the inevitable, unbiased conclusion is that a believer can indeed fall away from the faith, and that the wrath and eternal judgment of God awaits all those who refuse to repent of their sin and rebellious deeds. All the weight of Divine Writ bears forth the Truth that no one, believer or unbeliever, can elude accountability for his deeds:

> Or do you think lightly of the riches of His kindness and forbearance and patience, not knowing that the kindness of God leads you to repentance? But because of your stubbornness and unrepentant heart you are storing up wrath for yourself in the day of wrath and revelation of the righteous judgment of God, who will render to every man according to his deeds: to those who by perseverance in doing good seek for glory and honor and immortality, eternal life: but to those who are selfishly ambitious and do not obey the truth, but obey unrighteousness, wrath and indignation. There will be tribulation and distress for every soul of man who does evil...but glory and honor and peace to every man who does good...For there is no partiality with God. (Rom. 2:4-11)

"But, God Is Love!"

Inevitably, when you start talking about matters of judgment and believers falling away, proponents of eternal security will begin to cite scriptures concerning God's love, kindness, mercy, and patience. Of course, all these qualities are an inherent part of God's nature in boundless measure. Yet, scriptures proclaiming those Divine Attributes can never be used as a counterclaim against the validity of other scriptures concerning Divine Judgment. Scripture never contradicts itself. No passage of Scripture refutes or nullifies another.

What is difficult for the finite, humanistic mind to comprehend is that God's wrath and eternal judgment are not contradictory to His Divine Nature of Love, but an inherent part of it. Righteous indignation and wrath are an inherent part of the Righteousness of God. They are a part of Divine Love. As the last scripture quoted, Romans 2:4-11, indicates, the rich kindness and forbearance and patience of God is intended to lead people to repentance, not to give license to their continuance in sin. But, those who refuse to repent from their sin because of their "stubbornness and unrepentant heart" are only "storing up wrath" for themselves for "the day of wrath and revelation of the righteous judgment of God." And, on that Day of Wrath and Judgment, God will "render to every man according to his deeds." Those who have done good will inherit Eternal Life. Those whose deeds were evil will inherit wrath and righteous indignation.

"But, We're Saved by Grace!"

Another counterclaim often levied by proponents of the eternal security doctrine is that we are saved by grace. They misuse such scriptures as, "For by grace you have been saved through faith...not as a result of works, that no one should boast" (Eph. 2:8,9) for support of their ideology, and to counter scriptures concerning the judgment of apostate believers.

Of course everyone is saved by grace through faith, but we must never misconstrue the grace of God for license to sin, something which the Apostle Jude warned that "ungodly persons" do:

> For certain persons have crept in unnoticed, those who were long beforehand marked out for this condemnation, ungodly persons who turn the grace of our God into licentiousness and deny our only Master and Lord, Jesus Christ. (Jude 4)

God's grace is that "while we were still helpless, at the right time Christ died for the ungodly" (Rom. 5:6). We all were the "ungodly" for whom Christ died, though we in no wise deserved or merited it. That is God's grace.

God's grace is not a license to sin. Because God has through Jesus' shed blood justified us with Himself, does that mean He did it so that we could be permitted to continue in sin? Never! "Shall we sin because we are not under law but under grace? May it never be!" (Rom. 6:15). Or, "Are we to continue in sin that grace might increase? May it never be! How shall we who died to sin still live in it?" (Rom. 6:1,2).

It is true that we are saved by grace through faith. But, once we are saved we should "bring forth fruit in keeping with repentance" (Mat. 3:8). Our deeds should give proof of our salvation. As James said, "faith without works (*deeds*) is dead" (Jas. 2:17). The Amplified Bible translates that passage this way: "So also faith if it does not have works (*deeds and actions of obedience to back it up*), by itself is destitute of power — inoperative, dead." (italics added by author)

In other words, if we have truly been "saved by grace through faith," then our lives will be living testimony of that faith. Again, The Amplified Bible says it well:

> What is the use (*profit*), my brethren, for any one to profess to have faith if he has no (*good*) works (*to show for it*)? Can (*such*) faith save (*his soul*)? (Jas. 2:14, italics added by author)

Of course, the understood answer to that question is that such a "faith" is not the real faith through which one is saved. Such a "faith" that is void of corresponding good works cannot save anyone.

Second Corinthians 5:17 says, "Therefore if any man is in Christ, he is a new creature; the old things passed away; behold, new things have come." For a person to be "in Christ" means that he has surrendered his life unto the Lord, and has been saved by grace through faith. That person is "a new creature" because "the old things," the sinful deeds of the carnal nature are passing away through repentance, and are being replaced with the "new things," the godly deeds and behavior of the Born Again nature.

Are we saved by grace through faith? Of course we are. But, the grace of God is not a license to sin. The substitutionary sacrifice of Jesus Christ does not in any wise extend to justify the sin of those who "go on sinning willfully after receiving the knowledge of the truth" (Heb. 10:26).

No one, professing believer or unbeliever, who continues to practice willful sin will ever enter into Heaven, for:

> nothing unclean and no one who practices abomination and lying, shall ever come into it. (Rev. 21:27)

> But for the cowardly and unbelieving and abominable and murders and immoral persons and sorcerers and idolaters and all liars, their part will be in the lake that burns with fire and brimstone, which is the second death. (Rev. 21:8)

Last Days Apostasy

There are multitudes of people today who are in this second category of hearers of the Word of God, who because of insufficient repentance are like "rocky ground." When adversity arises against them, because they are only "temporary" believers, they fall away. And, adversity of many sorts is exactly what many believers are experiencing today.

In its own way, these last days in which we live are very difficult times, even for Christians. As the Living Bible says it, "in the last days it is going to be very difficult to be a Christian" (2 Tim. 3:1). Sin has run its course in perverting the entire Creation of God, from the condition of humanity itself, to the air Man breathes, to the Earth he inhabits. Thus, every element of the world in which we live has been corrupted down to the very foundation. The consequence is the effects of sin — adversity and tribulation.

However, the fire of testing is bringing purification to individual true believers and to the collective Body of Christ. The true wheat is being separated from the chaff, the *temporary* believers are being separated from the *eternal* believers. Purification is the result when true believers go through adversity, which is the reason God does not eradicate it entirely from their lives. Temporary believers, on the other hand, fall away as a result of afflictions and persecutions. The Lord Himself has testified concerning this, saying, "Behold, I have refined you, but not as silver; I have tested you in the furnace of affliction" (Is. 48:10).

In the same last days in which God is pouring out His Spirit upon all mankind (Joel 2:28), and multitudes are coming into the Kingdom of God, at the same time, many temporary believers are falling away from the faith. Many of them continue to attend church services, however, masquerading behind a facade of piety while their personal lives and behavior is as apostate as can be. As Jude said of such false brethren: "These men are those who are hidden reefs in your love feasts (*worship services*) when they feast with you without fear" (Jude 12, italics added by author).

Yet, this last day apostasy has not come upon us unawares. Jesus Himself prophesied it would happen, saying, "And at that time *many* will fall away" (Mat. 24:10, italics added by author). The Apostle Paul also echoed that prophesy through the same Spirit, and even added some insight as to what and who will motivate people to fall away in these last days: "But the Spirit explicitly says that in later times some will fall away from the faith, paying attention to deceitful spirits and doctrines of demons" (1 Tim. 4:10).

In the past, some theologians have surmised that this last day's apostasy would occur in some sort of a prevailing "a-religious" climate. However, the Apostle Paul indicated in the passage just quoted that those who would fall away in the last days would do so not because of being "a-religious" or antireligious, but because they were indeed "paying attention," only to the wrong spirit. Instead of paying attention to the Holy Spirit, they would be paying attention to deceiving religious spirits of Satan, and to religious doctrines concocted and propagated by demons.

Thus, while church people look for some great, contemporaneous, concerted mass defection from Christianity, multitudes of ultra-religious and pious-appearing church- goers are being surreptitiously led astray from the Truth as they pay attention to the deceitful religious spirits and erroneous doctrines of demons. And, it's all happening right under the noses of those church people and clergymen.

Israelite Example

As mentioned earlier, there are quite a number of scripture references and examples of people falling away. One prime example is the case of the Israelites. Their supernatural deliverance from the bondage of Egypt and subsequent supernatural sustenance during their forty year trek through the wilderness toward the Promise Land was all supernaturally orchestrated and accomplished by the Lord Himself. Yet, they repeatedly defected from their pledge of faith in the Lord during those forty years. They often wanted to return to the bondage of Egypt instead of espousing the freedom of serving the Lord, and even fashioned and worshiped false gods which they could see.

Finally, their persistent apostasy provoked God to anger. He swore they would never enter into the Promise Land because of their disobedience and disbelief. In His righteous wrath and judgment, God allowed that entire generation to be destroyed in the wilderness without ever entering in to the Promise Land, all except the only two men of an estimated million plus who believed God, Joshua and Caleb.

The Apostle Paul said this whole case of the Israelites was "written for our instruction." He repeatedly referred to it as his prime example of the falling away of people who had been saved by God. Here are some key passages of some of those references:

> Now these things happened to them as an example, and they were written for our instruction, upon whom the ends of the ages have come. Therefore, let him who thinks he stands take heed lest he fall. (1 Cor. 10;11,12)

> Take care, brethren, lest there should be in any one of you an evil, unbelieving heart, in falling away from the living God. (Heb. 3:12)

> Therefore, let us fear lest, while a promise remains of entering His rest, any one of you should seem to have come short of it. (11) Let us therefore be diligent to enter that rest, lest anyone FALL through following the same example of disobedience. (Heb. 4:1,11)

The Apostle Jude also alluded to the example of the Israelite apostasy and its consequences in his short but powerful letter. At the outset, Jude says that while it was his intention to write about "our common salvation," he was rather compelled to write instead "appealing that you contend earnestly for the faith." His exhortation closely paralleled that of the Apostle Paul in the same regard: "Fight the good fight of faith" (1 Tim. 6:12). Certainly, if Christians could not lose faith, neither of these eminent apostles would have written what would then be irrelevant exhortations, aside from the fact that God would certainly not have included it in His Word, of which nothing is superfluous.

Jude explained that the reason he was diverted by the Spirit to address this other topic was that there were "certain persons" who had:

> crept in (*to the fellowship of the saints*) unnoticed, those who were long beforehand marked out for this condemnation, ungodly persons who turn the grace of our God into licentiousness and deny our only Master and Lord, Jesus Christ. (Jude 4; italics added by author)

Jude forthrightly declared such ungodly, licentious people "were long beforehand marked out for this condemnation." He asserts that such people are indeed "condemned," and then he goes on to describe "**this** condemnation" as comparable to that of the Israelites:

> Now I desire to remind you, though you know all things once for all, that the Lord, after saving a people out of the land of Egypt, subsequently destroyed those who did not believe. (Jude 5)

Notice that Jude was reminding the saints that it was "**after**" God had "saved" the Israelites out of the land of Egypt that he "subsequently destroyed those who did not believe." As the Apostle Paul said, "these things happened to them as an example" to US, and the whole thing was recorded for posterity "for OUR instruction" (1 Cor. 10:11). The typological instruction given to us through the Israelite example is that Christians, those who have been saved out of the world (Egypt), subsequently, can be spiritually destroyed, and lose their rightstanding and fellowship with God (The Promise Land), if they fall away from faith in Christ Jesus.

The Angelic Example

But, Jude did not stop with the Israelite example. He strengthened his case even further by alluding to the fact that even a third of the angels fell away into utter apostasy with the high treason of Lucifer:

> And angels who did not keep their own domain, but abandoned their proper abode, He has kept in eternal bonds under darkness for the judgment of the great day. (Jude 6)

The Example of Sodom and Gomorrah

Jude even went on to associate the fate of these ungodly, licentious pseudo-Christians with that of the people of Sodom and Gomorrah:

> "Just as Sodom and Gomorrah and the cities around them, since they in the same way as these indulged in gross immorality and went after strange flesh, are exhibited as an example, in undergoing the punishment of eternal fire." (Jude 7)

Legalism: Galatian Type of Apostasy

In his letter to the Galatian church, the Apostle Paul rebuked and reproved them for reverting back to Judaistic legalism. He asserted that when people fall back under religious legalism after receiving salvation based on grace through faith in Jesus Christ, they actually sever their relationship with Christ and forfeit salvation by grace: "you have been severed from Christ, you who are seeking to be justified by law; you have fallen from grace" (Gal. 5:40).

The Galatian church made the grave mistake of reverting back to trusting in adherence to Jewish Laws in order to gain rightstanding with God, *after* they had been saved on the basis of undeserved favor which came through faith in Jesus Christ. Judaizers had infiltrated the Galatian church, propagating the false doctrine that once you are saved, you still must obey all the Jewish Laws and customs. (Unfortunately, some so-called "New Testament" Judaism sects are deceiving people today also with such ridiculous claims and bondage.)

The Apostle Paul was incensed and dumbfounded as to how the Galatian church which had understood "the meaning of Jesus Christ's death as clearly as though I had waved a placard before you with a picture on it of Christ dying on the cross" (Gal. 3:1, L.B.), could possibly become so deceived. They had actually cut themselves off from God through this legalistic form of apostasy. Paul's entire motivation in this letter was to rebuke, reprove, and to restore those who would repent back into fellowship with God. The following passages from that letter are key elements of the case he presented. The Living Bible rendition is quite good and understandable:

> ...some so-called "Christians" there — false ones, really — who came to spy on us and see what freedom we enjoyed in Christ Jesus, as to whether we obeyed the Jewish laws or not. They tried to get us all tied up in their rules, like slaves in chains. But we did not listen to them for a single moment, for we did not want to confuse you into thinking that salvation can be earned by being circumcised and by obeying Jewish laws. (Gal. 2:4,5)

...we Jewish Christians know very well that we cannot become right with God by obeying our Jewish laws, but only by faith in Jesus Christ to take away our sins. And so we, too, have trusted Jesus Christ, that we might be accepted by God because of faith — and not because we have obeyed the Jewish laws. For no one will ever be saved by obeying them. (Gal. 2:16)

Rather, we are sinners if we start rebuilding the old systems I have been destroying, of trying to be saved by keeping Jewish laws, for it was through reading the Scripture that I came to realize that I could never find God's favor by trying — and failing — to obey the laws. I came to realize that acceptance with God comes by believing in Christ. (Gal. 2:18,19)

I am not one of those who treats Christ's death as meaningless. For if we could be saved by keeping Jewish laws, then there was no need for Christ to die. (Gal.2:21)

Did you receive the Holy Spirit by trying to keep the Jewish Laws? Of course not....if trying to obey the Jewish laws never gave you spiritual life in the first place, why do you think that trying to obey them now will make you stronger Christians? (Gal. 3:2,3)

...those who depend on the Jewish laws to save them are under God's curse....Consequently, it is clear that no one can ever win God's favor by trying to keep the Jewish laws, because God has said that the only way we can be right in his sight is by faith....How different from this way of faith is the way of law which says that a man is saved by obeying every law of God, without one slip. But Christ has brought us out from under the doom of that impossible system by taking the curse for our wrongdoing upon himself. (Gal. 3:10-13)

So Christ has made us free. Now make sure that you stay free and don't get all tied up again in the chains of slavery to Jewish laws and ceremonies. Listen to me, for this is serious: if you are counting on circumcision and keeping the Jewish laws to make you right with God, then Christ cannot save you....Christ is useless to you if you are counting on clearing your debt to God by keeping those laws; you are lost from God's grace. (Gal. 5:1-4)

In the same letter, the Apostle Paul also destroys the counterclaim to the possibility of a Christian falling away based on Jesus' promise to never leave or desert us. Without at all being contradictory, Paul asserted that it is quite possible for believers to desert Jesus with his assessment that the Galatians had done precisely that: "I am amazed you are so quickly deserting Him who called you by the grace of Christ" (Gal. 1:6).

The subsequent verses also admonished against deserting Christ by following after a varied and distorted Gospel, like the one of legalism which deceived the Galatians, or like the one of "eternal security" by which so many are duped today:

> I am amazed that you are so quickly deserting Him who called you by the grace of Christ, for a different gospel; which is really not another; only there are some who are disturbing you, and want to distort the gospel of Christ. But even though we, or an angel from heaven, should preach to you a gospel contrary to that which we have preached to you, let him be accursed. (Gal. 1:6-9)

Bona Fide Believers?

Some of those who espouse the eternal security doctrine, in view of such scriptures as the ones cited in this chapter, retort that these are references to people who so-called "fall away" because they really are not true believers in the first place. They contend that these people only feigned their initial commitment. Thus, they had not actually fallen away.

However, that theory simply does not hold water. It is most definite that *someone* is falling away, because the Word of God says so. Besides, it is quite elementary that one must actually be "in" something to even be able to "fall away" from it.

Yet, even beyond all that, there is at least one particular scripture that completely explodes this theory. The following passage proves beyond the slightest doubt that a person can be truly saved and a partaker of all the fruits of redemption, and yet *then* fall away. This one is a real clincher. Eternal security proponents are never able to conjure up even a slightly reasonable counterclaim against this scripture.

> Hebrews 6:4-8
> 4 For in the case of those who have once been enlightened and have tasted of the heavenly gift and have been made partakers of the Holy Spirit,
> 5 and have tasted the good word of God and the powers of the age to come,
> 6 and then have fallen away, it is impossible to renew them again to repentance, since they again crucify to themselves the Son of God, and put Him to open shame.
> 7 For ground that drinks the rain which often falls upon it and brings forth vegetation useful to those for whose sake it is also tilled, receives a blessing from God;
> 8 but if it yields thorns and thistles, it is worthless and close to being cursed, and it ends up being burned.

It is astounding to see in this passage just how extensive a person's Christian experience can be, how many wonderful blessings and benefits they can receive, and then still fall away from their relationship with the Lord Jesus Christ. In versus four and five, Paul lists all the fruits of redemption of which these people had partaken. In a nutshell, they "got all there was to get."

In verse four, Paul says they were first of all, "enlightened," which meant they had consciously perceived the revelation of the Gospel of Jesus Christ, something which can only be effected through the illumination of the Holy Spirit. That in itself testifies of the validity of these peoples' experience, because the Holy Spirit does not enlighten false believers, and He cannot be fooled as to who is true and who is false.

Next, Paul reveals these people "have tasted of the heavenly gift and have been made partakers of the Holy Spirit." This is incontrovertible proof-positive that these people were indeed saved. "The heavenly gift," of which they had tasted is true salvation, for the Word of God says, "the gift of God is eternal life" (Rom. 6:23). Plus, the fact that they were "partakers of the Holy Spirit" really seals it, because the Holy Spirit only avails Himself to true, repentant believers. Unbelievers simply cannot be partakers of the Holy Spirit:

> "that is the Spirit of truth, whom the world cannot receive, because it does not behold Him or know Him, but you know Him because He abides with you, and will be in you." (Jn. 14:17)

Not only were these people "partakers of the Holy Spirit" in regards to the regenerative work and indwelling of the Holy Spirit, but they had also received the "baptism in the Holy Spirit," through which they experienced "the powers of the age to come" mentioned in the next verse. That experience, separate from the regenerative work of the Holy Spirit, is also available exclusively to bona fide believers. Bogus believers simply cannot receive the baptism in the Holy Spirit. Only true, Born Again believers can receive it.

In verse five, Paul says these people also had "tasted the good word of God." Like those in all four categories of hearers in Jesus' Parable of the Sower, these people had definitely heard the Word of God, and were by no means ignorant concerning it. Indeed, Paul says they were indeed "enlightened" to the Word. Moreover, they had to have heard and understood it in order to have been saved.

Then, the Apostle Paul says in the same verse that these people had also tasted even of "the powers of the age to come." This is a reference to the power which Jesus said Born Again believers would receive when the Holy Spirit came *upon* (not "in," but "*upon*") them when they received the Baptism in the Holy Spirit: "but you shall receive power when the Holy Spirit has come UPON you" (Acts 1:8). Through this experience adjunctive to salvation, believers are empowered to operate the nine supernatural gifts of supernatural power of the Holy Spirit (1 Cor. 12:8-10) via the unction of the Spirit. This power which is available to all believers is indeed "the powers of the age to come" which can be "tasted" of now in this age.

Still, incredibly, after partaking of all those magnificent benefits of redemption, these people subsequently fell away, according to verse six. They had been saved, were given Eternal Life, received the Indwelling and Baptism of the Holy Spirit, heard the Word of God, and had received an activation of the supernatural power of God. Yet, they still fell away.

The primary reason they fell away is precisely the point of this part of Jesus' parable as well as this book, which is that such people fall away because they are like "rocky ground" still full of the rocks of sin. They have not fully repented. Thus, they are still carrying out the deeds of the old nature. In this passage, God says by their sinful and apostate lives "they again crucify to themselves the Son of God, and put Him to open shame." This is God's view of what a person does when he has been saved by God and subsequently returns to a life of sin.

Another clue to these individuals' downfall is found in the word used twice in this passage — "tasted." Perhaps that was their shortcoming they should have "feasted" on instead of having merely "tasted" of all these spiritual provisions from God.

Renewal Impossible

In verse six of the same text, God explicitly says that in the case of these people who have fallen away "it is impossible to renew them again to repentance." It is not a matter of God not wanting to receive them back into fellowship with Himself, but that they can never again come to the point of true repentance in deed, which is a mandatory requirement for obtaining fellowship with God. On His own part, God is not desirous that anyone be banned from fellowship with Him and perish. However, all must come to repentance in order to obtain fellowship with Him. It is impossible for Him to have fellowship with those who unabatedly continue to participate in the unrighteous deeds of darkness, for "what partnership have righteousness and lawlessness, or what fellowship has light with darkness?" (2 Cor. 6:14). The incontrovertible and immutable fact is that genuine fellowship and communion with God is contingent upon genuine repentance.

It is so very sad as well as hard-sounding to say, but the people described in these passages have passed the point of no return and entered a kind of spiritual "twilight zone" in that they can never again get themselves to repent, and thereby loose themselves from the throes of sin, and return to God. God would certainly receive them if they could, but they simply can't, though, like Esau, they seek for repentance in deed with tears of remorse (see Heb. 12:17).

Now let it be clear: we are not talking about backsliding here — there is a difference between backsliding and falling away. Though it need not be that way, *many* sincere believers have come to the harsh realization some time in their lives that instead of growing and maturing, they had actually backslidden. In varying degrees, they had somewhat "left their first love" and had allowed their love for the Lord to "wax cold." Some are neither hot nor cold, but just "lukewarm," the kind of person Jesus said He will vomit out of His mouth (Rev. 3:16). If a backslidden person will but repent, and "remember therefore from where (he has) fallen" (Rev. 2:5) and confess his sin, God will forgive him or her.

These hearers mentioned in the Parable of the Sower are not mere backsliders, however. No, these people have completely and totally fallen away, and therewith have "again crucif(ied) to themselves the Son of God, and put Him to open shame." They have denied, rejected, and spiritually "crucified" Jesus by reneging on their previous acceptance of Him as their Lord and Savior and their commitment to serve and obey Him.

As in the case of the first three categories of hearers in the Parable of the Sower, though these apostate believers "have tasted the good word of God," they nonetheless do not bring forth any godly fruit from the Word in their own lives. The consequences of that is tragic and terrifying. Using again the simile of "ground" for believers, God says, ground that drinks the rain of spiritual blessings which God showers upon it "and brings forth vegetation useful to those for whose sake it is also tilled," will receive a blessing from God (Heb. 6:7). However, if it only yields spiritual "thorns and thistles, it is worthless and close to being cursed, and it ends up being burned" (Heb. 6:8), which means their final judgment will be to be cast into the everlasting fires of Hell.

Personal Experience

The most unfortunate part of cases such as those described in this passage in Hebrews is that there really are people like that. It has been my unfortunate experience to personally know, know of, and to have ministered to many people who have gone precisely this way. They have passed the point of no return. Like Esau, they have sold their birthright, who "afterwards, when he desired to inherit the blessing, he was rejected, for he found no place for repentance, though he sought for it with tears" (Heb. 12:17).

I have personally witnessed the cases of people who knew they would be "rejected" from Eternal Life and Heaven if they did not turn away from their sin, but who could not come to the place of actual repentance in deed, though they sought for it with tears of remorse. They rejected Jesus' offerings after once having had fellowship with Him, and publicly shamed Him by their lives of apostasy and sin. By and by, the bonds of sin tightened its grip on them, and their minds eventually became depraved, preventing them from being able to come to the place of actual repentance though they sought for it with rivers of tears of remorse.

The Apostle Peter knew well of these gone-astray former believers. He said they had become "accursed children; forsaking the right way they have gone astray, having followed the way of Balaam, the son of Beor, who loved the wages of unrighteousness" (2 Pet. 2:14,15).

In saying they had become "accursed children, forsaking the right way," he was indicating they were formerly children of God who had become accursed, "anathema," because they subsequently forsook the "right way." It is self-evident that in order to forsake it, they must have formerly been following the right way. He also said "they have gone astray," which intrinsically means they must have once been true sheep in the Flock of God in order to go astray from it.

Then, Peter goes on in his dissertation to make some comments concerning these fallen away believers that very aptly describes their plight:

> For if after they have escaped the defilements of the world by the knowledge of the Lord and Savior Jesus Christ, they are again entangled in them and are overcome, the last state has become worse for them than the first. For it would be better for them not to have known the way of righteousness, than having known it, to turn away from the holy commandment delivered to them. It has happened to them according to the true proverb, "a dog returns to its own vomit," and, "A sow, after washing, returns to wallowing in the mire." (2 Pet. 2:20-22)

A Final Example From Jesus

Jesus Himself gave us some enlightenment into this matter of the possibility of Christians falling away. One primary example is contained in a section of Scripture from which we have already quoted often. It begins with Jesus exhorting everyone to "Enter by the narrow gate; for the gate is wide, and the way is broad that leads to destruction, and many are those who find it" (Mat. 7:13). In the next verse, He gives us an indication of the exactitude of the true Christian walk in terms quite dissimilar to the "easy-gospel" preached by many today: "For the gate is small, and the way is narrow that leads to (Eternal) life, and few are those who find it."

In the subsequent six verses, Jesus talks about false believers, and how to recognize them by their fruit. And then, He gets to the real bottom line of this section:

> Matthew 7:21-23
> 21 Not everyone who says to Me, "Lord, Lord" will enter the kingdom of heaven; but he who does the will of My Father who is in heaven.
> 22 Many will say to Me on that day, "Lord, Lord, did we not prophesy in Your name, and in Your name cast out demons, and in Your name perform many miracles?"
> 23 And then I will declare to them, "I never knew you; depart from Me, you who practice lawlessness."

Some misguided people contend that if a person merely professes Jesus as Lord they are saved and are assured of going to Heaven. They go around so-called "witnessing," buttonholing people based on the idea that if they can badger them into repeating a prayer and merely saying Jesus is their Lord, then those people are "saved," and no matter what happens, they are going to Heaven, "because they confessed Jesus as Lord." But, that is NOT the way it is!

Indeed, the very point of Jesus' admonition in this passage is that that most certainly is not the way it is. In verse twenty-one, He specifically warns, not everyone who merely calls Him "Lord, Lord," will enter into Heaven. Mere verbal profession of Christ is not the criteria upon which fellowship with God and entrance into Heaven is granted. Rather, it is obedient performance of the "will of My Father who is in Heaven" (v. 21). Talk is cheap. It is the "doers of the Word" who are justified before God (Rom. 2:13).

Yet, according to verse twenty-two, these people described in this passage, are not people who just made some by-rote or mindless confession. These people were definitely saved at one point. We can know that with absolute certainty because they had received the "dunamis" power (Acts 1:8) of God to prophesy, cast out demons, and to perform *many* miracles, which are all manifestations of the supernatural power of God that are operable only by means of the unction of the Holy Spirit. This enablement is only given to Born Again believers through the gift of the Baptism in the Holy Spirit.

Parenthetically, it is important to note here that these people did legitimately perform these supernatural feats. But, it was not through the "power of the devil" as some people ignorantly and blasphemously contend. Evidence of that is found in these people's words to Jesus in which they rightly say they did these things "In YOUR Name." It was not done in the name or through the power of the devil, but in the name of Jesus. Moreover, Jesus did not refute either that they performed these deeds or that they were done in His name and behalf.

Permit me, if you will, to make one more point regarding another parenthetic issue here. Some people become quite disturbed and do not understand how people like these can continue to be channels of supernatural power from God if they are indeed fallen away in their personal conduct. In answer to that, let me point out that the Word of God forthrightly declares, "the gifts and callings of God are irrevocable" (Rom. 11:29). Once God gives a person supernatural gifts, and anoints and appoints someone into set-apart ministry, He does not subsequently revoke those gifts when they go astray spiritually. Besides, as evidenced by the case of the prophet Balaam being rebuked by his donkey, God reserves the Sovereign right to use any vessel He chooses.

However, Eternal Life and rightstanding with God is not predicated or dependent on one's gifts and accomplishments. The manifestation of God's power through these people was certainly a good thing, especially to its intended recipients. God is most desirous that people be beneficiaries of His supernatural power, and His usual modus operandi is to channel it through believers who make themselves available to Him. However, operation of these works of power had no bearing whatsoever on these people being qualified or disqualified from Eternal Life and entrance into Heaven.

In verse twenty-three, Jesus revealed the reason these people were rejected was because they practiced "lawlessness." They disobeyed God's Laws. They did not fully repent, or we could say they subsequently repented from their repentance after repenting. They did not just "slip up a little" or experience a momentary lapse as all of us have, rather they actually "practiced" lawlessness. They persistently practiced ungodliness. They willfully rejected godliness and holiness. So God rejected them and banned them from Heaven and Eternal Life.

Instead of receiving the approval and commendation Jesus will give every faithful believer on that day, in which He will say, "well done, thou good and faithful servant," these people will receive Jesus' terrifying command of eternal judgment: "Depart from Me, you who practice lawlessness."

Summary

The message of this portion of Jesus' parable, which focuses on the second category of hearers, those who are like "rocky ground," is to exhort believers to make a complete repentance, to renew their mind according to the Word of God, and allow the Lord to restore their soul through the sanctifying power of the Holy Spirit. Otherwise, those who refuse, foolishly toy with the possibility of falling away, and ending up in an apostate condition, unfit for and disqualified from the Kingdom of God, having become a "castaway." As the Word says, "Take care, **Brethren**, lest there should be in any one of **you** an evil, unbelieving heart, in falling away from the living God."

However, at the same time, if a believer will successfully complete this second step to bringing forth the fruit of Eternal Life, surrendering his entire life unto obedience of God and His will, he shall secure for himself Eternal Life by grace through faith in Jesus Christ. The believer who does these things need never concern himself about his salvation, for he is eternally secure, indeed:

> ...for as long as you practice these things, you will never stumble (*lit., fall away*); for in this way the entrance into the eternal kingdom of our Lord and Savior Jesus Christ will be abundantly supplied to you. (2 Pet. 1:10,11, italics added by author)

Part Five: The Third Category of Hearer

Chapter Ten

Those With Thorns

Mark 4:7,18,19
7   And other seed fell among the thorns, and the thorns came up and choked it, and it yielded no crop.
18   And others are the ones on whom seed was sown among the thorns; these are the ones who have heard the word,
19   and the worries of the world, and the deceitfulness of riches, and the desires for other things enter in and choke the word, and it becomes unfruitful.

In the preceding chapter, we discussed the category of hearers who fell away from the Lord before they were able to mature to the fruit bearing stage. This third category of hearers, those with the thorns, however, are significantly different from the former in that these believers did successfully complete the second step, and did survive to the stage of maturation in which they could bear fruit.

Still, these people also did not bring forth fruit because they had thorns growing in their lives which choked the Word and prevented it from producing any godly fruit.

In nature, the farmer must be sure to burn off any thorns and weeds that may be growing in the field he is going to seed, and take measures to prevent the growth of thorns all during the development of the crop until it is harvested. Otherwise, any thorns and weeds allowed to grow would choke out the crop, or at least seriously impair the yield.

Jesus used this allegory to indicate what happens in the spiritual realm. The thorns are "thorns of worldliness," which Jesus defined as being: 1) the worries of the world, 2) the deceitfulness of riches, and 3) the desires for other things. He said these thorns entered into these believers' lives, and choked out the Word as the two grew together, and prevented the Word from becoming fruitful.

As we have already discussed, the Word of God is designed to and has the power to bear fruit. God Himself is watching over His Word to ensure that it does bring forth its intended fruit (Is. 55:11; Jer. 1:12). Given the proper conditions in which to develop, it will constantly bear an increasing yield of spiritual fruit: "...the word of truth, the gospel...is constantly bearing fruit and increasing" (Col. 1:5,6).

God's desire has always been that Man be fruitful and productive. He charged the first Man, Adam, "Be fruitful and multiply, and fill the earth, and subdue it; and rule...over every living thing that moves on the earth" (Gen. 1:28). He was not just talking about procreation, but also about bringing forth the deeds and effects of righteousness upon the Earth.

Jesus came into the world to restore those who would believe in Him to the original estate of righteousness in which Adam lived before his fall. Now, God charges those Born Again believers, the redeemed, to bring forth fruit.

> I am the vine, you are the branches; he who abides in Me, and I in him, bears much fruit. (Jn. 15:5)
>
> You did not choose Me, but I chose you, and appointed you, that you should go and bear fruit. (Jn. 15:16)

People like those described in Part Four, those with "rocky ground," are not willing to make a complete surrender unto the Lordship of Jesus Christ, and eventually prove to be only temporary believers. They are not willing to "pay the price" for Eternal Life. Consequently, when tribulations come to test the validity and extent of their commitment, they fall away before they become spiritually mature enough to bring forth fruit.

This third category of hearer, however, is willing to pay the price of enduring the afflictions and persecutions which come their way. That was not their downfall. They made it through that stage of development. In fact, they made it all the way to the fruit-bearing stage of maturity. They were now at the stage in which they should bear some spiritual fruit. But, unfortunately, these people do not bear any fruit either. The reason they did not bear fruit is the subject of this part of the Parable of the Sower and this book.

Worldliness

One of the greatest problems with professing believers today is worldliness. There is nothing that will stunt a believer's spiritual growth and choke the Word of God in his or her life more than worldliness.

The Word of God renders a heavy indictment regarding those who are friends of the world and practitioners of its ways. James declared it was spiritual adultery:

> You adulteresses, do you not know that friendship with the world is hostility toward God? Therefore whoever wishes to be a friend of the world makes himself an enemy of God. (Jas. 4:4)

He bluntly states if you are a friend of the world, you are "an enemy of God," plain and simple. One person whose enemy I do not want to be is God.

The Apostle John also gave some strong, straightforward warning against worldliness, saying that anyone who loves the world simply does not love God:

> Do not love the world, nor the things in the world. If anyone loves the world, the love of the Father is not in him. For all that is in the world, the lust of the flesh and the lust of the eyes and the boastful pride of life is not from the Father, but is from the world. And the world is passing away and also its lusts; but the one who does the will of God abides forever. (1 Jn. 2:15-17)

The Apostle Paul informed us that the only way we can experientially prove the will of God in our own lives is to refrain from conformity to the world and to be "transformed" instead of being "conformed" by the renewing of our minds:

> And do not be *conformed* to this world, but be *transformed* by the renewing of your mind, that you may prove what the will of God is, that which is good and acceptable and perfect. (Rom. 12:2; emphasis added)

You see, this world is traveling a certain course, a carnal, ungodly course, leading to Hell. In Ephesians 2:2, the Apostle Paul called it "the course of this world." He said it was devised by Satan, "the prince of the power of the air," and motivated by "the spirit that is now working in the sons of disobedience." That "spirit" is the rebellious carnal nature of Satan himself, into which all of mankind is born in the natural birth. It is the "spirit of disobedience."

Following this ungodly course, traveled by the mainstream of the people of this world, is what "worldliness" is. Conformity with the world is worldliness. Espousing the ideals of the world is worldliness.

No one can follow after and be conformed to the course of this world, and have fellowship with God at the same time. As James said, "friendship with the world is hostility toward God." Godliness and worldliness are like oil and water — you can stir them up forever, but they will never mix.

Jesus said it was intrinsically impossible for anyone to serve two masters at the same time. A person's "master" is the one he serves and obeys (Rom. 6:16). Only two spiritual masters exist: Jesus and Satan.

God is Master of those who will obey and serve Him. Satan is automatically god of the people of this world (2 Cor. 4:4).

Jesus said, "you cannot serve God and mammon" (Lk. 16:13). "Mammon," by the way, does not just mean money, but all the trappings of this world. It really is "the things in the world" which John alluded to in the passage quoted earlier (1 Jn. 2:15). Jesus said a person simply cannot serve both the things of the world and God, "for either he will hate the one, and love the other, or else he will hold to one, and despise the other" (Lk. 16:13).

This was the downfall of this third category of hearers. They tried to serve both God and the world. They wanted to serve God, but they didn't want to detach themselves from the world to do it. They did not heed John's warning, and they still loved the things of the world. Thus, as Jesus warned, they ended up "hating" God in comparison to their love for the world. They tried to serve God and still "hold to" the world. Instead, in God's view, they "despised" Him.

Worldliness took its toll on these believers. It rendered them spiritually sterile, non-productive. In the next three chapters, we will examine the three "thorns of worldliness" that choked the Word and prevented it from bearing fruit in the lives of these believers.

Chapter Eleven

Thorn #1: Worries of the World

The first "thorn of worldliness" Jesus mentioned was "the worries of the world," which we will examine in this chapter.

Now each of these thorns of worldliness is in itself a very involved topic which would require an entire volume to expound upon in depth. However, that is not our purpose here. Rather, our purpose is to see how it is that each of these thorns of worldliness chokes out the Word of God and causes it to be unfruitful in the lives of believers.

"Cares of the Age"

As we examine this text, especially in the original language, some very interesting and significant points become manifest. First of all, it should be said that a more literal translation of the phrase rendered "worries of the world" in some modern versions would be: "cares of the age." The Greek word used here is *"merimna,"* which could be translated as *"cares,"* though it is a reference to concerns about which many people do indeed "worry." "Merimna" literally means *to draw in different directions*, or *to distract*. That is precisely what the worries of the world do — draw believers in different directions and distract them from the Word of God. But the most significant meaning of "merimna" is to "choke" — more on that later.

The Greek term translated *"world"* is also quite interesting. It is *"aionos,"* which actually connotes a specific period of time, an *"era,"* or an *"age."*

In effect then, the phrase constructed in the original language around *"merimna"* and *"aionos"* actually refers to the cares or concerns especially pertinent to the current era, hence: *"the cares of the age."* And, indeed, every particular era or age throughout history has had its cares and concerns that were especially indigenous to that age. This modern era is no different — it has cares and concerns that were not even existent in those preceding it. People of the Apostle Paul's era, for instance, did not have to concern themselves with many of the things that concern people living in the present era, such as a plethora of super-sophisticated, super-complex electronic gadgetry and communication media, international financial markets, the looming threat of nuclear warfare, environmental pollution, so-called "global warming" or even such now mundane matters as motorized land, air, and space travel.

Humanly speaking, it is no wonder that people do naturally tend to worry so much. In this age especially, everyone is confronted with an abundant range of concerns which directly affect his or her life. Most of us are not consciously aware of how many different concerns each of us have in the normal course of life. Let's look at some, which we will list under the two general categories of: personal and interpersonal concerns.

Just the usual personal concerns are numerous. We have physical personal concerns, which have to do with the care of our physical bodies. Some of those are: diet, hygiene, rest, sex, recreation, appearance, clothing, and shelter. There are emotional, mental, spiritual, vocational, financial, and educational concerns. Then, there are concerns regarding the ever-looming prospect of sudden calamity and catastrophe, criminal assault or other acts, accident, and physical disease, sickness, and impairment, which would also be included among the "worries of the world."

On top of all those personal concerns and cares indigenous to this age, there are also interpersonal concerns involving relations and relationships with others. Some of these are: romantic, domestic, familial, social, religious, public, civic, and even political concerns on every level from local to international.

These are all concerns affecting the average person during his or her life, directly or indirectly, voluntarily or involuntarily. Everyone must deal with all these matters as a normal part of life. Yet, it is vital that we do not become worrisome and full of anxiety because of them. The believer should not allow himself to become anxious or worrisome or loaded down with the "worries of the world." Believers should not set their minds on the things of the world, in the first place. God's Word exhorts believers:

> If then you have been raised up with Christ, keep seeking the things above, where Christ is, seated at the right hand of God. Set your mind on the things above, not on the things that are on earth. (Col. 3:1,2)

Some synonymous or related words with the word *"worry"* are: anxiety, stress, distress, tension, nervousness, care, concern, anguish, disquiet, fear, apprehension, and hysteria. Among the most common synonymous verbs are: fret, fuss, fume, and stew. Synonymous transitives would include: disturbed, distracted, disconcerted, plagued, upset, annoyed, troubled, beset, vexed, and tormented. All these words aptly describe the nature of worry.

Worry is a tremendously destructive and oppressive force of the exact opposite nature of faith. It is actually unbelief, and produces the exact opposite results of faith. Worry is a result of fear, whereas peace is a result of faith. Faith comes by hearing the Word of God (Rom. 10:17). Fear, worry and unbelief come by concentrating on the word of the world inspired by the god of this world, Satan, instead of God's Word.

Worry is sin. The temptation to worry must be resisted as any other sin is resisted. The Bible says, "whatever is not of faith is sin" (Rom. 14:23). Worry is a nasty habit that seems to be so "natural" to most people. It seems so natural because it is an inherent part of the carnal nature, though, perhaps, certain people may be more prone to succumbing to it than others. The reason it is such a difficult habit for many people to overcome, and for some to even see they need to, is that it is indeed so natural and such a common practice of the human specie (the only specie of life which practices it).

Some people have been "programmed" to worry. Some have been "raised" to worry. "Worry wart" parents have often taught their children the "fine art" of being a "worry wart." In a sense, with some people it is hereditary — if one of your parents was a "worrier," chances are, you will be one also, until you overcome it in Christ Jesus.

To the carnal mind, worry somehow just seems to be the right thing to do. For some, it is almost an institution. There seems to be something "religious" about worrying. Some people certainly do it religiously. If you took worrying away from some people, they wouldn't have anything with which to occupy themselves. I have had people get downright indignant with me when I preached along these lines, contending they had "a right to worry."

Some people have ingrained in them the idea that if they are not worrying, they are not "taking their responsibilities seriously." Well, certainly we are not to shirk our responsibilities. But, worrying about them will not help anything. In fact, persistent worry will only produce the exact adversity we are worrying about. As Job said: "For what I fear comes upon me, And what I dread befalls me" (Job. 3:25). And, God's Word cannot not work for us when we worry because it only operates through faith.

Adverse Effects of Worry

Constant anxiety is a very destructive and oppressive force, as I stated before. The adverse effects it produces are virtually innumerable, and can affect virtually every facet of a person's life. It can cause nervous, emotional, physical, and mental problems. It can adversely affect every kind of relationship, especially one's spiritual relationship and condition.

Numerous physical problems are sometimes attributed in whole or part to anxiety, such as: arthritis, heart trouble, hypertension, cancer, drug and alcohol addiction, gluttony, and a multitude of others. Many psychological problems are also sometimes caused, or at least compounded, by anxiety: fear, insomnia, mental illness, insanity, depression, suicidal tendency, paranoia, and other personality problems.

Prescription

By nature, worry is actually a spiritual problem, not physical, or even mental, even though its effects extend into so many other areas. Its basic cause is a "Word shortage," an inadequate intake of the Word of God. Faith dispels worry, and faith comes by hearing the Word of God (Rom. 10:17). If a person will feed his spirit upon the Word of God, and resist the habit of worry, it will begin to be broken and to dissipate. Then, instead of worrying about circumstances, "the cares of the age," that person will begin to believe God, and he can begin to apply the spiritual force of faith instead of the negative spiritual force of fear and unbelief.

The Bible tells us to "be anxious for NOTHING." In other words, God is actually telling us we are not to be filled with anxiety or worry with regard to ANYTHING. The King James Version even goes so far as to say that we should "be CAREFUL for nothing," which literally means we are not to be full of care concerning anything. Now that is a concept that to be sure is quite novel and completely foreign to many people, as it indeed was to me before I received Jesus into my heart. Some people worry and are anxious and filled with cares concerning just about EVERYTHING. But, God's Word tells us we should not permit ourselves to be caught up in worry, anxiety, and apprehension about anything. Instead, we are to commit all our cares unto God:

> casting the whole of your care — all your anxieties, all your worries, all your concerns, once and for all — on Him; for He cares for you affectionately, and cares about you watchfully. (1 Pet. 5:7, Amp. B.)

The passage that tells us not to be anxious about anything, goes on to tell us that instead of *worrying* about things, we should *pray* about them:

> Philippians 4:6-8
> 6   Be anxious for nothing, but in everything by prayer and supplication with thanksgiving let your requests be made known to God.
> 7   And the peace of God, which surpasses all comprehension, shall guard your hearts and your minds in Christ Jesus.

8   Finally, brethren, whatever is true, whatever is honorable, whatever is right, whatever is pure, whatever is lovely, whatever is of good repute, if there is any excellence and if anything worthy of praise, let your mind dwell on these things.

Verses six and seven tell us, if we will resist anxiety, and pray instead, making specific requests to God, and do it with advance thanksgiving, knowing that we have been granted the requests we have asked of Him according to His will (1 Jn. 5:14,15), then in the place of anxiety, we will enjoy peace of heart and mind, a peace that is beyond all human understanding.

Verse eight is one of a number of passages that instruct us to be selective regarding what we allow our minds to dwell on. It says if a thought is not true, honorable, right, pure, lovely, of good repute, excellent, and worthy of praise, we should not allow our minds to dwell on it.

In another passage along the same lines, the Apostle Paul declares that we must in effect annihilate, or bring to nought, every speculative and sophistic thought which exalts itself against the true knowledge of God:

> We are destroying speculations and every lofty thing raised up against the knowledge of God, and we are taking every thought captive to the obedience of Christ. (2 Cor. 10:5)

Though we often hear people say, "I have a hundred things on my mind," the truth is we really only entertain one thought at a time. This passage instructs us to take each individual thought "captive," and measure it up against the true knowledge revealed to us from God in His Word. Any thought not harmonious with the knowledge of God should be destroyed, annihilated, expelled from our thought process.

The consensus of Scripture is that believers should not allow themselves to be caught up in worry and anxiety about all the "cares of the age." We should leave the "worries of the world" to "worldlings." Believers should not set their minds on such worldly things, and must not be worldly-minded.

We should keep our minds fixed on the Truth, the Word of God, and the good promises of God, not on the lies of Satan, the word of this world, which worldlings speak. Instead, we should be "fixing our eyes upon Jesus, the author and perfecter of faith" (Heb. 12:2). Then, with our gaze fixed on Jesus and not on the worries of the world, we can trust God for our every need with peaceful hearts and minds.

When you do not cherish the things the world cherishes, you won't have your mind set on the things of the world, and you won't be caught up in the worries of the world. When you stop following the course of this world, and put Jesus first, His Kingdom and His righteousness, then you will not have any worries concerning the temporal things of this world. Paul summed it up well: "And do not be conformed to this world, but be transformed by the renewing of your mind" (Rom. 12:2).

Jesus Himself had these things to say regarding the worries of the world:

> Do not be anxious then, saying, "What shall we eat?" or "With what shall we clothe ourselves?" For all these THINGS the Gentiles eagerly seek; for your heavenly Father knows that you need all these THINGS. But seek first His kingdom and His righteousness; and all these THINGS shall be added to you. Therefore, do not be anxious for tomorrow; for tomorrow will care for itself; each day has enough care of its own. (Mat. 16:31-33)

> For what is a man profited if he shall gain the whole WORLD, and lose his own soul? or what shall a man give in exchange for his soul? (Mat. 16:26)

> Be on guard, that your hearts may not be weighted down with dissipation and drunkenness and THE WORRIES OF LIFE, and that day come on you suddenly like a trap. (Lk. 21:34)

Worry Chokes the Word

The paramount reason we should ensure against allowing ourselves to become caught up in the worries of the world is the reason Jesus cited in the Parable of the Sower: they "enter in and choke the word, and it becomes unfruitful" (Mk. 4:19).

This statement by Jesus, because of the particular words He used, was even more meaningful to His listeners who understood the Greek language because, as I mentioned at the beginning of the chapter, the Greek word for "worries" is "merimna," one of the literal meanings of which is *to choke*. It also means *to draw in different directions*, or *to distract*. Thus, Jesus was quite literally saying that when believers allow themselves to become caught up in these "cares of the age," along with the other "thorns of worldliness," they will become distracted and drawn in different directions by them, the ultimate result of which will be that these thorns will *choke out* the Word of God in our lives, preventing it from bringing forth the fruit it is intended to produce, even though we may be avid and attentive *hearers* of the Word.

Ultimately, regardless of the quantity and quality of our *hearing* of the Word of God, "the worries of the world," if they are present in our lives, will prevent us from being "effectual **DOERS**" of the Word, and it is not the hearers of the Word who are justified before God, but the "effectual **DOERS**" of it (Jas. 1:25).

Certainly, the consequences for not bearing fruit, as we will see later, are far too great to allow "the worries of the world" to render us spiritually barren "hearers" only "who delude themselves" (Idem). Therefore, let us all begin to practice what the Word says, and "be anxious for **NOTHING**."

Chapter Twelve

Thorn #2: Deceitfulness of Riches

The second "thorn of worldliness" which Jesus said would choke the Word of God and prevent it from bearing fruit in the life of its hearers is "the deceitfulness of riches." Of paramount importance, however, as we discuss this matter, is the fact that He did not say *riches themselves* were a thorn that would choke the Word of God and prevent it from bearing fruit, but rather "the DECEITFULNESS of riches."

Indeed, before we delve into the deceitful characteristic of riches and how it will choke the Word, it is somewhat vital that we lay to rest a fairly common misconception among uninformed or misinformed religious people. The essence of this rather widespread myth is that God is somehow opposed to the idea of Christians having money, at least in any significant amount, that God does not want believers to prosper, and that somehow to be truly spiritual one must be poor or at least only barely have his needs met.

We hear of the requirement of ministers in some denominations to take "a vow of poverty." Moreover, the preaching of some ostensibly pious people makes it sound as if God wants to take everyone's money away from them, leaving them poor and destitute. As a result, some people, ignorant of what the Word of God really says regarding the matter of money and other practical matters, have been led to believe that in order to become a Christian they would have to sell their possessions and give all their money away to the poor. Erroneous teaching based on half-truths has caused multitudes of sincere Christians to believe God wanted them to live in near abject poverty, and to fear ever having any money, "because, you know, money is the root of all evil."

Well, nothing could be further from the Truth. First of all, the Bible does not say money is the root of all evil. It says, "the **LOVE** OF MONEY is the root of all evil" (1 Tim. 6:10). God is by no means opposed to Christians having money, but He is totally opposed to covetousness. To put it another way, God is not opposed to believers possessing possessions, but He is entirely opposed to possessions possessing believers. The love of money and the pursuit of riches will prevent a person from loving and serving God, for:

> No servant can serve two masters; for either he will hate the one, and love the other, or else he will hold to one, and despise the other. You cannot serve God and mammon. (Lk. 16:13)

The Word of God is full of passages telling us just how much God desires for His children to prosper. In 3 John 2, He says, "Beloved, I wish above all things that thou mayest prosper, and be in health even as thy soul prospers" (KJV). What an amazing statement this is! Think on that for a moment and allow it to sink in. God is saying that above everything else He desires for us, and the Bible is replete with all the wonderful things He desires for us and our well-being, above all those things God wishes that we prosper financially.

Now the surpassing wisdom of God is demonstrated in this statement, which is that it is absolutely essential that we prosper financially in order to prosper physically in our body (i.e., health-wise) and spiritually in our soul (i.e., psychologically and emotionally). In other words, to be able to truly prosper in all the other aspects of our lives — spiritual, psychological, emotional, and social — it is imperative that we prosper financially.

I do not mean we all must be wealthy to live happily, but what is inherent in this morsel of Divine Truth is the unequivocal fact that financial prosperity is a requisite for real, maximal happiness. Continuous financial lack is a severely oppressing force that absolutely precludes us from living full, fulfilled, and truly happy lives, not only because of the lack of "things" that without question do make life more pleasant, but also because of the lack of capacity to do the things, such as helping others who are in need, that bring us pleasure.

The inexorable oppression of never-ending poverty has no rival, and to many is unbearable. Long-term, enduring financial lack in the case of untold multitudes has led to extreme physiological, psychological, and emotional problems, as well as ultimately to premature death either by means of physical disorders or, in the case of those whose pain was overwhelming, even suicide. God knows all this concerning the importance of financial wellness to our overall well-being, so it is His desire that we prosper financially, incredibly, "above all things."

Psalm 35:27 tells us to "CONTINUALLY" say, "The Lord be magnified, who DELIGHTS IN THE PROSPERITY OF HIS SERVANT," which is a far cry from what some people continually say. The truth is that God takes great delight in the prosperity of those who truly are His *servants*. When believers prosper through serving the Lord, God is glorified.

Another enlightening scripture says, "The Lord delighted over you to prosper you" (Deut. 28:63). Moreover, in this same chapter God repeatedly indicates that poverty is a part of the curse of disobedience, and that prosperity, not poverty, is a part of the blessings of obedience, which stands in stark contrast to the postulations of some pseudo-spiritual people who preach just the opposite — that prosperity is a curse and poverty is a blessing.

Poverty is in no way a "blessing," as anyone who has suffered it can tell you, if they are honest about it and don't come up with some pseudo-spiritual hogwash about how it "helped their faith" or something. According to the Word of God (and His Word is far more trustworthy than that of people like that), faith does not come by *poverty*, it comes by hearing the Word of God (Rom. 10:17). Anything to the contrary is poppycock. Poverty, when a person gets tired enough of it, may motivate him or her to do a little more of the Word, which in turn will produce more faith, but poverty itself is not going to help, increase, or activate your faith one iota; never has, never will. Rather, unabated poverty will ultimately produce precisely the opposite of faith.

God says if we will obey His voice and commandments, He will elevate us "above all the nations of the earth. And all these BLESSINGS shall come upon you and overtake you...the Lord will make you abound in PROSPERITY" (Deut. 28:1-11). Again, we see here that prosperity is a blessing of obedience to God.

In the infamous case of Job, he started out very rich, and after a period of reproof from God with respect to his blatant fear and lack of faith and trust in God, God made Him even richer, twice as rich as a matter of fact. Careful and unbiased study of his story will prove that contrary to his now infamous exclamation, "The Lord gave, and the Lord hath taken away," it was not God who took away all his possessions and children, but rather Satan, who was able to do so because fear of loss had pervaded his life and eroded the protective hedge of faith in God (read Job 2). In retrospect, Job admitted, "For the thing which I greatly FEARED is come upon me, and that which I was afraid of is come unto me."

But, after being reproved by God through a face to face encounter with His Majesty Himself, a chastened Job exulted, "I know thou canst do all things...I have heard of Thee by the hearing of the ear; but now my eye sees Thee; therefore I retract, and I repent in dust and ashes." The result was that "the Lord restored the fortunes of Job...**twofold.**"

We can see from the story of Job that God is not in the business of chastening those who are serving Him by stripping them of their possessions and relegating them to poverty, as some people ignorantly allege. Rather, as Elihu, the only one of Job's counselors to speak truth to Job, declared, "If they obey and serve Him, they shall spend their days in prosperity" (Job 36:11).

Psalm 37:11 says, "The humble (*obedient*) will inherit the land and will delight themselves in abundant prosperity." And, verse nineteen essentially promises that even in famine conditions and economic chaos, the righteous "will have an *abundance*"(italics added by author).

The bottom line is that God does not want His children to be in want of anything that is a legitimate need. One passage so much as says that: "O fear the Lord, you His saints; for to those who fear Him, there is no want...they who seek the Lord shall not be in want of any good thing" (Ps. 34:9,10). Another favorite passage tells us because the Lord is our Shepherd, we "shall not want" (Ps. 23:1).

What kind of a father would take pleasure in seeing his children in constant want and need, especially of the essentials of life? Certainly our Heavenly Father does not want us to be in want. Jesus revealed the attitude of our Heavenly Father: "If you then, being evil, know how to give good gifts to your children, how much more shall your heavenly Father give what is good to those who ask Him" (Mat. 7:11).

The Apostle Paul succinctly summed up the whole matter in this one passage: "And my God shall supply ALL your NEEDS according to His riches in glory in Christ Jesus" (Plp. 4:19). God promises in this verse to provide ALL of our *needs*, not necessarily our *greeds*, but all our *needs*, and in so doing will not limit Himself to our puny Earthly resources, but will draw from His own limitless wealth of riches in glory. Wow! What a promise!

Deceitful Characteristic of Riches

Even the small sampling of passages I have mentioned here, well establishes the foundation that God does not require or even desire that believers live in poverty or financial lack, and provides us with more than ample Scriptural evidence to conclude without equivocation that it is not riches or wealth themselves that will prevent the Word of God from bearing fruit in a person's life. Rather, as Jesus indicated in the Parable of the Sower, it is the deceptive characteristic of riches that can cause tremendous spiritual problems and prevent the bringing forth of Godly fruit in a person's life, even those who have heard the Word of God. It is trusting in and coveting the riches that will choke the Word of God and prevent it from bearing the fruit it is intended to produce. As God says it, the LOVE OF MONEY is the root of all evil: which while some coveted after, they have erred from the faith, and pierced themselves through with many sorrows. (1 Tim. 6:10, KJV)

Riches can be so deceiving. Many a person has been deceived by riches. One of the worst parts of the deceptive nature of riches is a false sense of superiority. There is an arrogant and haughty spirit that can invade and pervade a person when wealth and the trappings of wealth are his quest and, in effect, his god. That haughty spirit is one of seven things that God absolutely loathes and considers abominations (Pr. 6:16,17); in fact, it is at the top of the list. Yet, sadly, many people are consumed with such a false sense of superiority predicated on their wealth.

Beyond that, many wealthy people are under the delusion they are somehow right with God simply because they are rich. The power, prestige, prominence, preeminence, and preferential treatment afforded the affluent in the world's system often produces a blind self-righteousness and elitism which leads to the wholly false assumption that they must also be right with God. However, monetary worth certainly does not impress God in the slightest, nor can it buy rightstanding with Him. Rightstanding with God can be gained by no other means than on the basis of grace through faith in the Lord Jesus Christ (Rom. 3:21-24).

High-standing in the Kingdom of God is not based upon monetary worth, but on servitude to others: "whoever wishes to become great among you shall be your servant; and whoever wishes to be first among you shall be the slave of all" (Mk. 10:43,44). There is no partiality with God, for He is no respecter of persons. It is for certain that one's financial status will be of no consequence on the day of judgment and one's wealth will produce no advantage, for: "Riches do not profit in the day of wrath" (Pr. 11:4).

"How hard it will be for those who have riches to enter into the kingdom of God," Jesus said (Mk. 10:23). He did not say it would be *impossible*, but that it would be *hard*, or difficult, for the rich to enter into the Kingdom of God. He did not say that it would be hard for true believers who have riches or who are wealthy to enter, because all true believers enter into the Kingdom by grace through faith in Christ, regardless of their wealth or lack thereof. Jesus is not talking here about believers having money, rather He is talking about unbelievers who have not yet entered the Kingdom of God, and how hard it will be for them to do so.

The reason it will be difficult for them to enter the Kingdom of God is this arrogance and pride to which I have already alluded. There is only one way for anyone, whether rich or poor, to enter the Kingdom of

God — by recognizing your utter spiritual poverty, that you are a totally lost and condemned sinner, and that you desperately need the saving of the Savior. Coming to that realization is often the stumbling block for the rich of the world, however. Pride prevents them from ever admitting the fact that, though they may have financial wealth and prestige in this world, when it comes to their spiritual condition, they are bankrupt and destitute. That is the essence of "the deceitfulness of riches," and many of the rich, unfortunately, have been deceived by it.

Jesus went on to say, "It is easier for a camel to go through the eye of a needle than for a rich man to enter the kingdom of God" (Mk. 10:25). Now Jesus' allegory here really was not of a camel passing through the eye of a literal needle, for that in reality would not be merely *difficult*, as Jesus said it would be for the rich to enter the Kingdom of God, but rather that would be altogether *impossible*.

Very familiar to His listeners, was something known as "the eye of the needle," which was a very short and narrow passageway in the wall surrounding Jerusalem. It was the only way into the city at night when the main gates were closed as a deterrent against enemy attack. Merchants returning home at night from their business forays, usually did not arrive back at Jerusalem until long after the main gates had been closed. When they did finally return, the only entrance into the city was through "the eye of the needle," through which both the merchant and his camels had to pass.

Now the passageway by design was only large enough to allow a man to barely make it through down on his hand and knees, which design precluded en masse attacks by marauders. It was difficult enough for a man to negotiate the entryway, but the merchant's camels also had to pass through the same portal. In order for the camels to be able to pass through "the eye of the needle," they would first have to be stripped bare of their cargo of wares which they had been carrying. Then, one at a time, with some firm prodding the merchant would coax the unwilling camels to bend down on their knees and to slowly crawl through the ever so short and narrow entrance.

Jesus said it was easier for those camels to pass through that tiny passageway, aptly dubbed "the eye of the needle," than for a rich person to enter into the Kingdom of God. For, you see, everyone must enter the Kingdom of God, the Heavenly Jerusalem, in the same manner the camel entered the Earthly Jerusalem, allegorically speaking, that is, stripped totally bare of all worldly possessions and merit, down on your knees in true humility, realizing you possess nothing with which to commend yourself to God and that you are entering only through the wholly unmerited acceptance afforded you only through faith in Jesus Christ, and with profuse, heartfelt, and eternal gratitude and thanksgiving.

Everyone must repent of their pride and false sense of superiority in order to enter the Kingdom of God, no longer glorifying and exalting their self, but glorifying and exalting the King of kings and Lord of lords, Jesus Christ. As James said, "Let the rich man glory in his humiliation" (Jas. 1:10). How fitting also is the admonition in this passage directed to those who have attained unto wealth in this life:

> Beware lest you forget the Lord your God by not keeping His commandments and His ordinances and His statutes which I am commanding you today; lest when you have eaten and are satisfied, and have built good houses and lived in them...then your heart becomes PROUD, and you forget the Lord your God....Otherwise, you may say in your heart, "My power and the strength of my hand made me this wealth." But you shall remember the Lord your God, for it is He who is giving you power to make wealth, that He may confirm His covenant which He swore to your fathers as it is this day. (Deut. 8:11-18)

Idolatry of Trusting in Riches

God says He is a "jealous God," and that we are to have no other gods before Him, and that we are not to make or serve any idols (Ex. 20:1-5). An idol, or false god, is something you attribute undue homage and affection to, or something you trust in and place your faith in and look to, to deliver you, and to help you overcome the adversities of life, and to attain unto personal desires, ambitions, and aspirations.

By that definition, money is the false god of multitudes of people in this world. This has always been true, but never more so than it is in this last day in which we live, something which was explicitly prophesied by the Spirit, "But realize this, that in the last days difficult times will come. For men will be lovers of self, LOVERS OF MONEY..." (2 Tim. 3:1,2). Money, however, is such a vain thing in which to trust. God says, "He who trusts in riches will fall" (Pr. 11:28). Riches are only temporal, they do not last forever. They can be here one day and gone the next, as the following scriptures indicate:

> For riches are not forever. (Pr. 27:24);

> Do not worry yourself to gain wealth, cease from your consideration of it. When you set your eyes on it, it is gone. For wealth surely makes itself wings, like an eagle that flies toward the heavens. (Pr. 23:4,5);

> Instruct those who are rich in this present world not to...fix their hope on the uncertainty of riches but on God. (1 Tim. 6:17);

> Let the rich man glory in his humiliation, because like flowering grass he will pass away. For the sun rises with a scorching wind, and with-

ers the grass, and its flower falls off, and the beauty of its appearance is destroyed; so too the rich man in the midst of his pursuits will fade away. (Jas. 1:10,11);

Come now, you rich, weep and howl for your miseries which are coming upon you. Your riches have rotted and your garments have become moth-eaten. Your gold and your silver have rusted; and their rust will be a witness against you and will consume your flesh like fire. (Jas. 5:1-3);

But godliness actually is a means of great gain, when accompanied by contentment. For we have brought nothing into this world, so we cannot take anything out of it either. (1 Tim. 6:6,7);

Do not lay up for yourselves treasures upon earth, where moth and rust destroy, and where thieves break in and steal. (Mat. 6:19)

Without realizing it, multitudes in the world today have made money their god. They trust in it to deliver them from every adversity of life, for personal validation and to give them a sense of dignity and rightness, to afford them prestige and preeminence, to garner for themselves the favor and deference society bestows upon the wealthy, and to provide them with a sense of security, satisfaction, and fulfillment. In a nutshell, people look to money and riches to give them the peace, happiness, contentment, and sense of general well-being to which people commonly aspire. It is in looking to money to supply all this, that people unconsciously make money their god, notwithstanding the adamant denials of most that they have done so in their own case.

But, it is Jehovah God who is the true Supplier of all these things, and He desires that people recognize Him as such. In fact, all these things can only be realized in their truest form through fellowship with God. To seek any other object or entity as a source of these things is idolatry, and is making a false god of that object or entity.

The love of money, or covetousness, which is idolatry, is a natural motivation of the carnal nature that is inherent within us all, however (Eph. 5:5; Gal. 5:19,20). In varying degrees, before we were saved and began renewing our minds according to the Word of God, we all trusted in money for all the things we are supposed to trust God to accomplish in our lives. Thus, most people commit their entire lives and energies in the quest to acquire more and more money, the more the better. They seem to think that the more diligent they are in the pursuit of it, the more favorable the false god of money will be to them. The more they have of it, the more it will deliver them from the adversities and tribulations of life, and fulfill the various yearnings of their heart. So they think.

How often have we all thought at one time or another in our lives, "If

I can just get this one bill paid off, then I just know everything will be alright." Or, "If I can just get that new car," or "that new house," or whatever, "I just know everything will be fine, then." Or, "If I can just save up $10,000 in my savings account," or "make this one great stock purchase," or "buy this new business," or "get that new job," or "that promotion," or "that raise," — "well, everything will be great then!"

That, my friend, like it or not, is idolatry. It is placing a false trust in money. It is making money your god. It is trusting in riches, and in your own power to make wealth. But, even more than all that, such reasoning indicates you have been deceived by "the deceitfulness of riches!" The truth of the matter is that once you do get that one bill paid off, you only get more and even larger bills to contend with, and everything is still not "alright." Or, have you ever noticed, after you buy that new house or car, everything is still not "fine?" Or you save up that $10,000, or purchase those stocks, or buy that new business, or you land that new job, or get that promotion or raise in pay, and then everything is still far from being "great?" Instead you have even more problems. That's the deceitfulness of riches; he who trusts in them is heading for a fall (Pr. 11:28).

You see, God does not want everything to be "alright" merely through the means of monetary gain and because of financial wealth. He does not want you to be trusting in money as your savior and deliverer. If you do, money is your master and god, not Him. God delights in the prosperity of His servants, but therein is the key: He wants our lives to be prosperous in every way, not through the self-glorifying means of self-achievement, but through serving Him, whereby all the glory for our prosperity is attributable to Him alone. He wants to be our total Source, our only Savior and Deliverer, our Master, and our very present Help in the time of trouble. He wants to be the object of our affection and trust.

The Consequences of Covetousness

The love of money, or covetousness, certainly is the root of all evil, and it causes a complete breach in one's fellowship with God. Jesus said, "Beware, and be on your guard against every form of greed; for not even when one has an abundance does his life consist of his possessions" (Lk. 12:15). As we have already seen, Paul said those who have coveted riches, often "have wandered away from the faith, and pierced themselves with many a pang" (1 Tim. 6:10). Hence, we can see that covetousness and greed can most certainly cause a believer to "wander away from the faith," that is, become apostate subsequent to salvation.

As Jesus said, no one can successfully serve two masters, God and money. He said that if you "love," that is, attribute your affections to and expend the vast majority of your energies pursuing, money, you in effect "hate" God. As the Apostle John put it, "If anyone loves the world, the love of the Father is not in him" (1 Jn. 2:15).

"Out of touch," irrational, and unduly harsh, these undeniably Biblical Truths are considered in this day when the pursuit of riches has come to be regarded as a wholly noble and honorable pursuit, and when Christians have become indoctrinated with the concept that materialistic obsession is even godly. Moreover, anyone who dares to preach such concepts is subjected to scorn, ridicule, and contempt. Christendom today, for the most part, has lost sight of or does not want to recognize the Truth that covetousness is still sin for which there is a penalty if it is not repented from. The unadulterated Truth is this: anyone who fails to repent of covetousness will ultimately end up out of fellowship with God, will be disqualified from Eternal Life, precluded from inheriting the Kingdom of God, and banished from Heaven unto eternal judgment. The following scriptures trumpet forth warnings to that effect:

> "Or do you not know that the unrighteous SHALL NOT INHERIT THE KINGDOM OF GOD? Do not be deceived; neither fornicators, nor IDOLATORS, nor adulterers, nor effeminate, nor homosexuals, nor thieves, nor THE COVETOUS, nor drunkards, nor revilers, nor SWINDLERS, SHALL INHERIT THE KINGDOM OF GOD." (1 Cor. 6:9,10)

> For this you know with certainty, that no immoral or impure person or COVETOUS MAN, WHO IS AN IDOLATER, HAS AN INHERITANCE IN THE KINGDOM OF CHRIST AND GOD. Let no one deceive you with empty words, for because of these things THE WRATH OF GOD COMES UPON THE SONS OF DISOBEDIENCE. (Eph. 5:5, 6)

> Now the deeds of the flesh are evident, which are:...IDOLATRY...of which I forewarn you just as I have forewarned you that THOSE WHO PRACTICE SUCH THINGS SHALL NOT INHERIT THE KINGDOM OF GOD. (Gal. 5:19-21)

> But for the cowardly and unbelieving and abominable and murders and immoral persons and sorcerers and IDOLATERS and all liars, their part will be in the lake that burns with fire and brimstone, which is the second death. (Rev. 21:8)

Everyone should heed God's warnings concerning the deceitfulness of riches and covetousness, including and especially believers, since it will most definitely choke the Word and prevent it from bringing forth fruit. Probably no warning in this regard is more poignant than the one Jesus issued through the medium of the parable of the rich fool:

> And He said to them, "Beware, and be on your guard against every form of greed; for not even when one has an abundance does his life

consist of his possessions." And He told them a parable, saying, "The land of a certain rich man was very productive. And he began reasoning to himself, saying, 'What shall I do, since I have no place to store my crops?' And he said, 'This is what I will do; I will tear down my barns and build larger ones, and there I will store all my grain and my goods. And I will say to my soul, 'Soul, you have many goods laid up for many years to come; take your ease, eat, drink and be merry.' But God said to him, 'You fool! This very night your soul is required of you; and now who will own what you have prepared?' So is the man who lays up treasure for himself, and is not rich toward God." (Lk. 12:15-21)

God called this man "a FOOL." In his covetousness and greed he just stored up his goods, and as they increased, he merely built more barns to store up more goods. But, on the night his soul was required of him, he was spiritually bankrupt. He had stored up all his riches for himself, instead of being generous with it unto others in obedience to God. He was rich *toward himself*, but "not rich toward God." God said to him, "You fool!"

The Word of God tells us to "give" (Lk. 6:38), not to "store up." We are to be generous, giving to others who are in need and for the preaching of the Gospel. God Himself is generous, and is always giving. He gave the supreme gift of His only begotten Son, the best He had, to us for our salvation. A godly person, i.e., one who is like God, will also be a giving person. As a bonus, God says that whatever we give on behalf of Jesus unto the needy and for the sake of the preaching of the Gospel, will be returned to us in up to one-hundredfold measure, NOW in this life and age, and in the age to come we will have the reward of Eternal Life (Mk. 10:29,30).

Jesus taught that the way to keep from being covetous and deluded by the deceitfulness of riches is to lay up our treasures in Heaven by giving on His behalf here on Earth. If we are covetous and greedily store up here on Earth instead, it will be constantly subjected to depletion by various forms of "thieves break(ing) in to steal" and economic modulation. If we are generous givers here on Earth, however, we will be storing up treasures in Heaven. But even greater than that, we will be demonstrating where our heart and what our "treasure" really is — things in Heaven, or things on the Earth:

> Do not lay up for yourselves treasures upon earth, where moth and rust destroy, and where thieves break in and steal. But lay up for yourselves treasures in heaven, where neither moth nor rust destroys, and where thieves do not break in or steal; for where your treasure is, there will your heart be also. (Mat. 6:19-21)

Covetousness Not Exclusive to Rich

Having said all this concerning covetousness, it needs to be pointed out that there is a common misconception in this regard that covetousness is found exclusively among those who would be considered financially rich. But, that is a fallacy. You do not have to be rich to be covetous and caught up in the love of money. There are myriads with financial resources below the wealthy level who are covetous and deceived by the deceitfulness of riches. The fact is, there are many times more non-wealthy people who harbor covetousness in their hearts than there are those who are rich and covetous.

The harsh truth is that their covetousness is often the very thing that keeps the poor reeling under the cruel curse of never-ending poverty and financial lack. Sadly, the poor often stay poor because in their covetousness, or in some cases fear of lack, they never sow any financial seed, thereby precluding them from ever reaping a harvest. Those, on the other hand, who are generous givers, find the Law of Sowing and Reaping continually producing for them an abundant harvest that supplies their every need.

Summary

In bringing this chapter to a close, let me offer this summary concerning the second "thorn of worldliness." Do not be deceived by the deceitfulness of riches. Place all your trust in God the Father and His Son, Jesus Christ. Riches will fail you; God will never fail you. Riches are temporal, and only indigenous to this life; Jesus Christ is the True Riches of Eternity. Do not seek riches, "But seek first His kingdom and His righteousness; and all these THINGS shall be added to you" (Mat. 6:33).

Probably the best attitude concerning riches one can adopt is found in the Proverbs of Solomon: "Do not worry yourself to gain wealth, cease from your consideration of it"; and, "Give me neither poverty nor riches; feed me with the good that is my portion" (Pr. 23:4; 30:8).

If we will seek the Kingdom and righteousness of God rather than riches, the Word of God will not be choked by the worldly "thorn" of "the deceitfulness of riches," allowing it to produce the fruit of the Kingdom of God in our lives, that is, if we also remove from our lives the third thorn of worldliness — "the desires for other things." We examine that deadly thorn in the next chapter.

Chapter Thirteen

Thorn #3: Desires For Other Things

We have so far discussed two of the three "thorns of worldliness," which Jesus said would choke the Word of God and prevent it from bearing fruit in the lives of those who are hearers of it. We now come to the third and final thorn of worldliness — "the desires for other things."

Though to translate the Greek phrase as "the desires for other things" would not be incorrect, some further amplification is in order. The two base words of this phrase in the original language are: "epithumaia" and "loipa." Although some translations render the Greek word "epithumaia" as "desires," it more accurately denotes "lusts" or "strong desires." The Greek word connotes more intensity than the simple English word "desires." Several more apt English synonyms of "epitheumaia" may be: *lusts, cravings, drives, longings,* and *motivations.*

The other base word of this phrase in the original language is "loipa." It literally means "the remaining things." It connotes the things that are left, the rest, or the other things not already mentioned.

Thus, these two words coupled together in this text actually refer to all the other worldly distractions and strong desires not accounted for under the categories of "the worries of the world" and the "deceitfulness of riches." The Amplified Bible may best capture Jesus' intended meaning regarding this last thorn: "THE CRAVING AND PASSIONATE DESIRE FOR OTHER THINGS creep in and choke and suffocate the Word, and it becomes fruitless." I have personally come to believe this is more what Jesus is talking about here — the other worldly lusts, pursuits, motivations, and ambitions in which people often become immersed, consuming their time, attention, and energies, thus distracting them from the Word of God and godly pursuits.

Phillip's Modern English translation describes these other worldly desires as "all sorts of other ambitions," which "creep in and choke the life out of what they have heard." This is also a very apt interpretation of what Jesus was referring to here. Some of those "ambitions" that can "creep in and choke the life out of" the Word are: vocational pursuits, intellectual pursuits, avocations, entertainment, recreation, and the like.

In many cases, the objective of such involvement is self-gratification and self-exaltation of such forms as: fame, notoriety, recognition, power, adventure, ownership, social prominence, and so forth.

Everyone's life is by nature multi-faceted. We all have different pursuits into which we pour our energies, and rightfully so. Every functioning member of society must have a vocation through which to gain his sustenance and to occupy himself. Even avocations and recreation play an important role. These are all essential elements of human life.

However, none of these things should ever be ends in themselves. As an end in themselves, they only amount to "vanity and chasing after the wind," as Solomon said. They are only intended to be a means to an end. They do not possess the ability themselves to bring happiness, peace, and the fulfillment we all desire and require. God has so designed the order of life that these ends are only attainable as the blessings of fellowship with Him, the Creator of Life. When these ambitions and pursuits do become an end in themselves, they are vanity. Moreover, it consumes the person's energies, chokes the life out of the Word of Life in his own life, and distracts him from seeking first the Kingdom and righteousness of God. These things can take such preeminence in the lives of believers that they lose their godly perspective, and soon begin to compromise on the principles of the Kingdom of God in the vain quest to fulfill these ambitions and achieve these self-exalting goals.

In truth, such pursuits as an end are nothing more than means of self-gratification, which is to say, selfish ambition. The Word of God calls it *idolatry*. Those who practice such idolatry shall not inherit the Kingdom of God (1 Cor. 6:9,10; Gal. 5:19-21), but the wrath of God instead (Eph. 5:5,6). In fact, the Word straightforwardly declares the destination for all idolators will be "the lake that burns with fire and brimstone, which is the second death" (Rev. 21:8).

Thus, it is absolutely imperative that every true believer examine in all honesty his own life, to determine whether any of these vain, selfish ambitions have crept into his own life, distracting him from his "first love." Every believer must be extremely watchful, and not allow these "desires for other things" to creep into his life and to choke the Word, preventing it from bringing forth its intended fruit. In the end, we must all give account for own lives. We want to be among those to whom God will say, "Well done, thou good and faithful servant." We do not want to be among those worthless servants whose lives amounted only to "vanity and chasing after the wind," concerning whom Jesus will say, "cast out the worthless slave into outer darkness; in that place there shall be weeping and gnashing of teeth" (Mat. 25:30).

Chapter Fourteen

Removing the Thorns

Jesus indicated in the Parable of the Sower that "the worries of the world," "the deceitfulness of riches," and "the desires for other things," were all spiritual "thorns." If allowed to grow in a person's life, they will gradually, subtly, but eventually choke out the Word of God, and prevent it from bearing the fruit it is intended and has the power to produce. In the same way thorns are the enemy of crops in nature, so these "thorns of worldliness" are the believer's enemy and the nemesis to the Word of God within the life of a believer. Though many people try to make it so, and deceive themselves into thinking it *is* so, there is never a "peaceful co-existence" of worldliness and the Word in a believer's life, for these are two diametrically opposed forces. They are simply in no wise compatible.

In his typically straightforward way, James aptly declared, "whoever wishes to be a FRIEND of the WORLD makes himself an enemy of GOD" (Jas. 4:4b). And, essentially, is that not the gist of many people's problem? — they want to have God, salvation and all its benefits, Eternal Life and avoid eternal damnation in Hell, but they want the world too. As the saying goes, "they want to have their cake and eat it too."

But, it just does not work that way. One cannot be "friendly" with the world, that is, embrace its ways and desire its delicacies, and at the same time be "friendly" with God. Jesus made that clear when He declared,

> "NO ONE can serve two masters; for either he will hate the one and love the other, or he will hold to one and despise the other. You cannot serve God and mammon (*i.e., the world and it's ways and accouterments*)" (Mat. 6:24; italics added by author).

Again in this regard, James is blunt but clear: "You adultresses, do you not know that friendship with the world is hostility toward God?" (Jas. 4:4a). One may deceive himself into believing he or she is successfully maintaining a friendship with the world and with God at the same time, but it is delusion and an illusion. Many Christians sincerely believe they are successfully maintaining this balancing act of loving God and loving the world simultaneously, but God says that friendship with the world is actually "hostility" against God, because the two are entirely antithetical. Loving the world is hostility toward God.

Remember how James addressed people who were maintaining this friendship with the world "You adultresses,..." (Jas. 4:4a). In the heart of God, worldliness is spiritual adultery. God Himself unabashedly declared concerning Himself, "I, the Lord your God, am a JEALOUS God" (Ex. 20:5). So, there is such a thing as holy *Divine Jealousy*. Divine Jealousy demands that our love and affection for God be undivided and wholly dedicated. God's Word directs us, "Set your affection on things above, not on things on the earth" (Col. 3:2, KJV). After we have "married" ourselves unto God upon dedicating our lives to Him, and then afterwards carry on a love affair with the world, God considers that an adulterous relationship in which the world is our paramour or mistress. In so doing, we grieve the heart of God.

Moreover, not only is friendship with the world *adultery*, but it is *idolatry* as well, for it is attributing to someone or something else the affections that are supposed to be reserved for God. And, God's Word is clear that adulterers and idolators will have no part in the Kingdom of God: "Do not be deceived; neither FORNICATORS, nor IDOLATORS, nor ADULTERERS...shall inherit the kingdom of God" (1 Cor. 6:9,10).

Now in no way, though, does any of this mean believers are to become alienated and totally disenfranchised from the people of the world. It is vital to understand that there is a distinction between *the world* and *the people of the world*. True Biblical Christianity does not call us to religious estheticism and interrelational segregation from the people of the world, but rather indeed to be kind, loving, and uncondemning toward unbelievers. Moreover, it is they who we desire to reach with the Good News of the Gospel of Christ, and most people can sense alienation and hostility a proverbial hundred miles away. Remember, Jesus ate, fellowshipped, and interacted with sinners and those who did not accept Him as the Son of God and Messiah, for it was for those very people that He came and was crucified.

So when a person becomes Born Again, he or she must repent from all worldliness and cease from setting his or her affections on the ways and things of the world. The believer must extricate or remove from his or her life the three "thorns of worldliness" Jesus delineated in the Parable of the Sower. In essence, in so doing, the believer will be complying with the instruction to "not be CONFORMED to this world, but be TRANSFORMED by the renewing of your mind" (Rom. 12:2), so that he or she will no longer be comporting with the world's image of what humans should be and do, but rather will be conforming themselves to the Image of a genetic Son of God, as we are predestined by God (Rom. 8:29).

Notwithstanding, though believers are predestined to be conformed to the Image of the Son, until and unless one is Born Again, he or she has no choice but to live a life that is conformed to the world and its system. The way of the world is all the unregenerate person knows at that point, hence, he or she cannot be or live any other way.

Through no choice of our own, our initial, physical birth into this world is a fleshly birth into the order of carnality, into sin and spiritual death, because of the permeation of the human lineage with sin. Though with that physical, fleshly birth we become alive physically, we are nevertheless spiritually "dead in (our) trespasses and sins," and remain so until we are Born Again by accepting Jesus as our personal Savior. Thus, since we are spiritually dead, we have no other option but to follow "the course of this world," which is in accordance with "the spirit that is now working in the sons of disobedience," which is the carnal nature, which is "the spirit" of Satan, who is "the prince of the power of the air" (Eph. 2:1,2).

This carnality blinds and darkens the minds of the unbelieving (2 Cor. 4:4), or unregenerate, with regard to spiritual truths, so that all they know is the order of carnality which pervades this world of spiritual darkness. The consequence is that until we are regenerated by the infusion of the Life of God into our human spirit, we are not even able to comprehend the principles of the Kingdom of God, "being darkened in (our) understanding, excluded from the life of God, because of the ignorance that is in (us)" (Eph. 4:18).

However, when a person is Born Again, he is instantaneously and miraculously delivered from the domain of darkness, and is transferred into the Kingdom of Light, which is the Kingdom of God (Col. 1:13). At that point, the person who is Born Again is no longer a subject of the kingdom of darkness. Instead, he is then a subject and member of the Kingdom of God; this world is no longer his home, for his citizenship is in Heaven (Plp. 3:20). Once we are Born Again as a child of God, though, we are to begin the process of being transformed through having our minds renewed into conformity and concurrence with the Word of God rather than with the world as it had been formerly (Rom. 12:2).

Jesus Himself said believers are "*in*" the world but we are not "*of*" the world (Jn. 17:11,14-16, italics added by author). We are living in this world system on planet Earth, certainly, but as Born Again believers we are made partakers of the Divine Nature, and have therefore escaped the corruptions that are in this world by the agency of lust (2 Pet. 1:4,5). We have been emancipated from this world's order, from captivation to the carnal nature and bondage to its sinful lusts, and we no longer are compelled to conformity with this world order and the sin permeating it. Rather, we are free to be transformed by the renewing of our mind through the Word of God unto conformity with the Image of the Son of God (Rom. 8:29). Albeit, that by no means infers that such transformation is automatic, but only that the capacity and potential exists for the believer to become transformed and to become conformed to the Image of the Son of God through the renewing of his or her mind by means of the assimilation of and obedience to the Word of God.

Having been given that emancipation from the dictates, demands, and desires of the carnal nature as a result of the New Birth, it is imperative that every believer subsequently actually repent from worldly lusts, cares, ambitions, and desires. As discussed previously, the first message Jesus preached at the beginning of His public ministry was: "Repent, for the Kingdom of heaven is at hand" (Mat. 4:17). In saying this He meant that the Kingdom of Heaven was now attainable by all who would repent from sin and turn to Him, since He Himself was the Door into the Kingdom, and He had now come. Repentance is the act of turning around from going in one direction and then going in the opposite direction. Every believer must turn away from following after "the course of this world" (Eph. 2:2), that is, the world's ways, order, and system, and begin to follow Jesus Christ and the path of righteousness into which He guides us (Ps. 23:3) in order to enter the Kingdom of God.

Repentance from worldliness is not optional but mandatory. As someone has aptly allegorized, it is okay for the ship to be in the ocean, but if the ocean gets into the ship, it's in jeopardy of sinking. Likewise, it's okay for the believer to be in the world, but if the world gets into the believer, he's in jeopardy of sinking into apostasy. Just as a leaking ship will eventually be swallowed up by the same ocean that is leaking into it, so also a leaking believer will eventually be overcome by the worldliness leaking into his life.

The application of all this to the third category of hearers in the Parable of the Sower is that all believers must remove the "thorns of worldliness" from their lives, in order to be able to bear the Godly fruit they as children of God are intended to produce. They must repent from these worldly attitudes and ways and refuse to be affected by them any longer.

The following scriptures sum up so well all we have been discussing in this chapter regarding turning away from worldly attitudes and ways in order to begin following after God's Word, Will, and Ways:

Since you became alive...now set your sights on the rich treasures and joys of heaven where he sits beside God in the place of honor and power. Let heaven fill your thoughts; don't spend your time worrying about things down here. You should have as little desire for this world as a dead person does. Your real life is in heaven with Christ and God. (Col. 3:1-3., L.B.)

That is why you must kill everything in you that belongs only to earthly life: fornication, impurity, guilty passion, evil desires and especially greed, WHICH IS THE SAME AS WORSHIPING A FALSE GOD; all this is the sort of behavior that makes God angry. And it is the way in which you used to live when you were surrounded by people doing the same thing, but now you, of all people, must give all these things up...You have stripped off your old behavior with your old self, and you have put on a new self which will progress toward true knowledge the more it is renewed in the image of its creator... (Col. 3:4-10, L.B.)

In this new life one's nationality or race or education or social position is unimportant; such things mean nothing. Whether a person has Christ is what matters, and he is equally available to all. (Col. 3:11 L.B.)

Removing the "thorns of worldliness" from our lives is the third and final requisite mentioned in the Parable of the Sower for bringing forth in our hearts and lives the God-like fruit of the Kingdom of God. After having successfully completed these three steps of getting up on the road, removing the rocks of disobedience, and removing the thorns of worldliness, a believer then has the capacity to become like the fourth category of hearers, who are the only ones to bring forth fruit. This fourth category of hearers is the subject of the next chapter.

Part Six: The Fourth Category of Hearer

Chapter Fifteen

Those With Good Soil

Mark 4:8,20
8   And other seeds fell into the good soil and as they grew up and increased, they yielded a crop and produced thirty, sixty, and a hundredfold.
20   And those are the ones on whom seed was sown on the good soil; and they hear the word and accept it, and bear fruit, thirty, sixty, and a hundredfold.

Finally, we come to the last category of hearers of the Word. In a nutshell, they are the very antithesis of all the others. They are the only ones who bore fruit upon hearing the Word of God. The reason they bore fruit in itself is the "secret" to bearing godly fruit.

Jesus likened these people to "good soil." Their hearts were not like "*rocky* ground" or "*thorny* ground," but "*good* ground," representing acceptance and obedience of the Word. This was the simple differential that distinguished these hearers of the Word from all the others and made them "good" ground — "they hear the word and accept it," Jesus said. Their "secret" to bearing fruit was just that when they heard the Word, they accepted and obeyed it. They simply did what James exhorted us all to do: "receive the Word implanted which is able to save your souls," and became "doers of the Word" (Jas. 1:21,22).

In the case of this last category, everyone and everything involved did exactly what they were supposed to do. The sower sowed the Word, as he had in the case of the other categories. The Word itself stood ready and fully effectual to perform all it promised. However, the all important difference was that these hearers, unlike the others, received the Word implanted in the good soil of acceptance and obedience. Consequently, having been afforded the right conditions, the Seed was able to produce the fruit of the Kingdom of God in the lives of these hearers.

The Mystery of the Fruit-bearing Process Revealed

Jesus indicated as He explained this parable to the disciples that it contained the very "mystery of the kingdom" of God. He said everyone must understand this parable to be able to understand all the others. Yet, the "mystery" itself of how the Kingdom of God is procreated in a person's life is just this simple: the Word of God is the Seed that will reproduce the fruit of the Kingdom of God in the good soil of those who will hear, accept, and obey it. The "formula" for bearing fruit is really no more complex than that. The complexities regarding bringing forth fruit which do exist are produced by the sin nature and the demonic forces opposing the Kingdom of God, not the fruit-bearing process itself.

The focus of this chapter is the last category of hearers, who are characterized as "good soil." But, they are our focus because the fruit-bearing process, which is our transcendent concern, is culminated in them, and thus is embodied and revealed by them. Indeed, inherent within the very metaphorical moniker attributed to them, "good soil," is the gist of the fruit-bearing process, which is that the key lies in the nature and quality of the soil itself. In the preceding chapters, we defined, isolated, and examined the various components of the fruit-bearing process Jesus delineated in the Parable of the Sower. In this chapter, we see how all those various components come together, or culminate, in this last category of hearers. To attain unto that end, however, we need to take just a moment to briefly review the nature and role of the various elements, so that we can then pull them all together and see clearly how they all work together in concert.

The first element of the process is the Seed that is sown by the sower, which is the Word of God. The Word of God is the incorruptible "seed" (1 Pet. 1:23-25) by which we are Born Again, or spiritually regenerated, which effects our entrance into the Kingdom of God. It is the Seed of Kingdom-procreation by which the entire Kingdom of God is reproduced in believers. Our souls are saved, or restored and sanctified, by receiving this Seed implanted in the good soil of acceptance and obedience (Jas. 1:21). All our spiritual growth and maturity is brought about as we partake of the "pure milk of the Word" of God (1 Pet. 2:2). We are taught and guided by the Seed of the Word (Ps. 119:105). The Seed is even our healing, and we can be healed through the revelation of the Seed of the Word as it is implanted and develops within our spirits (Ps. 107:20). Not to mention the innumerable other benefits derived from the Word of God, which time and space obviously will not allow us to delineate here.

Suffice it to say that virtually everything of the Kingdom of God is appropriated through the Word of God. As we receive it, it effects the "mysterious" process of reproducing the Kingdom of God within our hearts and lives. And, all this is true concerning the Seed because the Seed is none other than Jesus Christ Himself in whom is the summing up (consummation) of all things "concerning the Kingdom of God."

Jesus is the literal Seed (Greek word: "sperma") of God, the only begotten genetic Son or Progeny of God. As we receive that sole genetic Sperma or Seed of God into our spirits we are spiritually procreated after the Image and Life of God and made into the "tekna" (Greek), or genetic offspring (progeny), of God (Jn. 1:12).

After sharing the Parable of the Sower with the disciples, Jesus went on to relate two other parables in which He likened the Kingdom of God to a "Seed." In the first, He emphasizes the fact that the Seed itself will reproduce the Kingdom of God in those who yield to its work, even though the sower does not know exactly how it is that the reproduction process works:

> And He was saying, "The kingdom of God is like a man who casts seed upon the soil; and goes to bed at night and gets up by day, and the seed sprouts up and grows — HOW, HE HIMSELF DOES NOT KNOW." (Mk. 4:26,27)

It is much like the electricity we all use every day. Few of us really understand how it works, we just know that it *does* work when we turn on a light switch or appliance. The reproduction of the Kingdom of God in our hearts and lives is accomplished by the power of the Word of God as it is sown into our spirits by hearing it (reading is a form of hearing). It is not necessary that we fully understand exactly how it works in order for it to work and to rely upon its effectuality, rather we just know that it does indeed work, and we *expect* it to work when we turn on the switch. If we will sow the Seed into our hearts, it will somehow reproduce the Kingdom of God in us. How it does it is the "mystery" of the Kingdom of God of which Jesus was speaking in the parable.

Jesus continued on to give further explanation as to how the crop is produced, saying that once the Seed has been cast upon the ground, the *soil itself*, which we have established represents acceptance and obedience, "produces crops BY ITSELF," which corroborates the assertion that it is the *soil* of those who hear the Word that determines whether or not the Seed will produce fruit as it has the ability and is intended to do:

> The SOIL produces crops BY ITSELF; first the blade, then the head, then the mature grain in the head. But when the crop permits, he immediately puts in the sickle, because the harvest has come. (Mk. 4:28,29)

In the next parable He related, Jesus likened the Kingdom of God to "a mustard seed":

> And He said, "how shall we picture the kingdom of God, or by what parable shall we present it? It is like a mustard seed, which, when

sown upon the soil, though it is smaller than all the seeds that are upon the soil, yet when it is sown, grows up and becomes larger than all the garden plants and forms large branches; so that the birds of the air can nest under its shade." (Mk. 4:30-32)

What this parable illustrates is the following. The Kingdom of God begins in our hearts as a very small Seed. Undoubtedly, Jesus used the allegory of a mustard seed, which is among the smallest of all plant-producing seeds, to illustrate the extreme relative smallness of the Seed of the Word of God compared to the looming magnitude of the many seeds of worldliness pressing about us seeking implantation in our hearts. Nevertheless, despite its comparative diminutiveness, given the conditions necessary for growth, the incorruptible Seed will in due season eventually grow to become the largest and most prevalent "plant" in our lives, and produce the fruit of the Kingdom of God.

The Six-step Fruit-bearing Process

Jesus reveals in the Parable of the Sower that bringing forth fruit is a process, more specifically, a six-step process which must be adhered to diligently. We see in the account of the first category of hearers that the first step of the process is to get up on the road of Eternal Life. This first category of hearers, who Jesus referred to as "those beside the road," *rejected* the Word of God, which in actuality is Jesus Himself, upon hearing it. They did not *receive* it so as to be saved. Instead, they totally *rejected* it, and thereby remained beside the road of Eternal Life. The opposite of that, of course, is to receive the Word, and as a person receives the Word of God as a Seed, he is Born Again by it, and gets up on the road of Eternal Life. So, step one is — get up on the road of Eternal Life.

Then, the next thing that must begin to happen after a person has accepted Jesus is that he must begin to remove the rocks of sin and carnality from his heart and manner of life, or conduct; this, in essence, is repentance. He must begin to repent of these former passions, desires, and deeds, thereby causing those "old things" to begin to pass away, allowing "new things" to come to replace the old (2 Cor. 5:17). In so doing, the new believer allows the Lord to effect the process of sanctification within his or her life, and avoids being one of the second category of hearers who were like "rocky ground," who are only temporary, "fair-weather" believers who immediately fall away into apostasy when persecution and affliction arise. Hence, step two is — get the rocks out of your life, or in other words, repent.

Next, after one has gotten up on the road of Eternal Life, has repented from the old life, and has removed the rocks of sinful conduct from his life, he then must allow the Lord to purify him even further by burning off the "thorns of worldliness," so that they do not creep in and choke the Word, and prevent it from bearing fruit. John The Baptist declared that Jesus would baptize us "with the Holy Spirit AND FIRE" (Mat. 3:11), a statement which has puzzled many. Drawing from a number of passages, the enigma is resolved, making it clear that the "fire" he mentioned was a figurative reference to the refinement fires of the purification process effected by the Holy Spirit in the life of every believer (1 Cor. 3:9-15). In the natural, as any farmer or horticulturist can tell you, the best way to remove thorns from a field is to burn them off. That is precisely what the Lord does in the lives of willing and sincere believers. As we come to the place of maturity wherein we can endure the dealings of the Lord in our lives without fainting, the Holy Spirit begins to purify us of the "thorns of worldliness" we discussed in the previous four chapters. So, step three for bearing fruit is to be purified from the thorns of worldliness.

Once a believer has performed these initial steps of the fruit-bearing process he or she will then have arrived at what can appropriately be called "the fruit-bearing stage."

Maturity: The Fruit-bearing Stage

The New Birth is the beginning of every believer's New Life. But it is just that — the beginning, not the culmination, as some people have erroneously believed. Subsequent to salvation, we must begin to "press on to maturity, not laying again a foundation" (Heb. 6:1).

Every believer's life must first be founded upon the only true foundation, the Lord Jesus Christ (1 Cor. 3:11), and that founding occurs with and at the moment of the New Birth. When a person is Born Again, the foundation of the nature and Life of Christ is laid within that person's regenerated spirit. As with the construction process in the natural, the laying of the foundation is a process of its own. The ground in which the foundation will be laid must be properly prepared by excavation to the requisite depth and removal of obstructions. Only then can the foundation be laid in accordance with the design.

But, the laying of the foundation is only the beginning of the construction process in the natural. In effect, the laying of the foundation is the precursor to the building of the building. After the foundation has been laid, the building of the actual building can then begin in earnest. So also is it with the spiritual building program: first, the foundation must be properly laid, which requires excavation and purging (repentance), and then, after the true and sure foundation of Christ, who is the Word of God, has been properly laid, the building of the building can commence, which must be constructed in exact conformity with the blueprint — the Image of Jesus (Rom. 8:29).

The spiritual foundation is and forever will be flawless and perfect, for it is the Life of Christ Himself, who is Perfection Personified. The problem is never with the foundation. Flaws, imperfections, and incongruities with the blueprint inherent in the spiritual building that is built are the sole result of how and what one *builds* upon that foundation following the New Birth.

That is the essence of this admonition: "Let EVERY MAN be careful how he BUILDS upon it (*i.e., the foundation*)" (1 Cor. 3:10, italics added by author). This means every believer, whether he knows it or not, subsequent to being Born Again, is building a building upon the foundation of Christ. That building is the substance and record of the life we live following the Rebirth, and the building of that building God deems *our* "work" (see below). One either constructs his or her building with the Godly building materials of gold (God-like attributes), silver (God-like love in deed toward others), and precious stones (labor and activity toward the establishment of the Kingdom of God) — all of which are made more precious by refinement fires, or that person is automatically building with the only other existing building materials, the carnal and Godless building materials of wood (mere human effort), hay (self-aggrandizement, self-interest), and straw (worldly, humanistic works) — all of which are consumed by fire. Moreover, God promises that EVERY person's life is going to be tested by fire to clearly and indisputably reveal which building materials he or she used to build his or her building upon the foundation.

All this is the essence and import of the following passage of Scripture:

> No man can lay a foundation other than the one which is laid, which is Jesus Christ. Now if any man builds upon the foundation with gold, silver, precious stones, wood, hay, straw, each man's WORK (the substance and record of one's life) will become evident; for the day will show it, because it is to be revealed with fire; and the fire itself will test the quality of each man's WORK. If any man's WORK which he has built upon it remains, he shall receive a reward. If any man's WORK is burned up, he shall suffer loss; but he himself shall be saved, yet so as through fire.

Thus, as the Hebrews 6:1 passage indicates, after the foundation is laid, one then begins to build upon that foundation.

The gradual, systematic construction of the building itself upon the foundation of Christ, in essence, is the maturation or maturing process of the building. Then, as the building is being constructed and we begin to come into spiritual maturity, we will be able to start bearing the fruit of the Kingdom of God that Jesus said we were chosen and appointed to bear. For, maturity is the fruit-bearing stage. Hence, the admonition, "let us press on to maturity."

God does not want believers to flounder around in spiritual infancy all their lives. He wants us all to mature, to grow up spiritually. He has already supplied the spiritual food necessary to grow spiritually, which is the Word of God: "like newborn babes, long for the pure milk of the word, that by it YOU MAY GROW in respect to salvation" (1 Pet. 2:2). The clear indication of this passage is that God requires that believers GROW in respect to salvation.

Nevertheless, for a large percentage of professing Christians, salvation alone is enough, and they make little to no effort to grow or to press on to maturity, and are at the minimum apathetic, and in some cases hostile, toward spiritual maturation. Sadly, multitudes of such believers remain spiritual babies, and are quite content to do so.

But, what is worse is that there are myriads of so-called "churches," which are really little more than spiritual "nurseries" who are wholly dedicated to the perpetual "care" of these supposedly "saved" people who have absolutely no desire to grow up and spiritually mature. Instead of requiring that believers spiritually mature, and developing and training them to become what they are supposed to become in order to produce the true spiritual fruit they are supposed to produce, these spiritual "nurseries" merely "babysit" the spiritual babies, keeping them occupied with interminable, innocuous church-games and fleshly interactivities designed to entertain and supposedly promote interrelationships (aka, "fellowship").

Indeed, in these "churches" the training program that does exist is designed to cause those under their "care" to remain spiritual babies, because that is all "nurseries" know how to do — take care of babies. Once babies or children grow up, they outgrow the "nursery" and its program, and, if they are to "press on to maturity," they must ultimately leave, which some eventually do. Their departure in turn necessitates they be replaced with other babies, if the nursery is to preserve and perpetuate itself.

Thus, in "churches" such as this, there is a never-ending cycle of attrition. Spiritual newborns are birthed in these "birthing wards," but they soon find it necessary to depart in order to progress to the next level of development and training in spiritual "homes" under the tutelage of spiritual parents who have the love, dedication, wisdom, and "spiritual parenting skills" to guide them toward spiritual maturation. That is, IF they are fortunate enough to find truly God-anointed "spiritual parents" who are genuinely endowed with the spiritual gifting for effectual spiritual rearing and development of spiritual "babes."

In essence, the entire "ministry" of these churches is designed to do the very thing Hebrews 6:1 explicitly says NOT to do, that is, "NOT laying AGAIN a foundation." Churches such as these are totally consumed with laying the foundation of salvation through acceptance of Christ, again, and again, and again, and again, ad infinitum. Indisputably, the foundation must be laid. But, once it is laid, we are then commanded to "press on to maturity," and not be perpetually occupied with laying the foundation over and over again. The church that obeys the command to lay the foundation is worthy of commendation, but transforms its *commendation* to *condemnation* with its failure to obey the command not to lay it again and to press on to maturity.

We have already seen God's exhortation to "press on to maturity" expressed through the Apostle Paul *(note: the authorship of Hebrews is debated by theologians)*. Just before that passage, Paul reprimanded the Hebrew believers for not growing out of their spiritual infancy into adulthood. He implied they were still spiritual "babes" because they still needed baby food and were not yet ready for "solid food":

> ...you have come to need milk and not solid food. For every one who partakes only of milk is not accustomed to the word of righteousness, for he is a BABE. But solid food is for the MATURE, who because of practice have their senses trained to discern good and evil. (Heb. 5:12-14)

There are so many professing Christians like that today also. They spend their whole lives gumming the baby food of elementary spiritual principles, never moving on to chew on the spiritual meat of weightier matters contained in the Word of God, and growing thereby. Pabulum is all they ever eat, so they remain spiritual babies.

The Apostle Paul chided the Corinthian church in a similar manner as well because they too had proved by their carnality that they were also still spiritual babies:

> And I, brethren, could not speak to you as to spiritual men, but as to men of flesh, as to BABES, in Christ. I gave you milk to drink not solid food; for you were not yet able to receive it. Indeed, even now you are not yet able, for you are still fleshly.... (1 Cor. 3:1-3)

In Ephesians, God reveals He has anointed certain believers with special ministry gifts to minister to the Body of Christ in order to bring it into spiritual maturity (Eph. 4:11-13). Then, He goes on to describe what the results of that should be:

> As a result, we are no longer to be CHILDREN...but speaking the truth in love, we are to GROW UP IN ALL ASPECTS INTO HIM, who is the head, even Christ. (Eph. 4:14,15)

It is vital for all believers to be constantly growing unto spiritual maturity. For one thing, growth is evidence of life, both in the natural and spiritual realm. Anything that is not growing is dying or dead. Spiritual growth is the evidence of spiritual life. If you are not growing toward spiritual maturity, though you are still alive, spiritually, you are dying and will end in spiritual death if the condition is not reversed. Moreover, the ultimate reason we must continue to grow and develop unto spiritual maturity is that, as we shall see in the following two chapters, God not only *desires*, but *requires* that every believer bear fruit, and maturity is the fruit-bearing stage. Nature tells us that is true, but affirmation is also inherent in one of Jesus' analogies concerning the Kingdom of God to which we referred earlier:

> And He was saying, "The kingdom of God is like a man who casts seed upon the soil; and goes to bed at night and gets up by day, and the seed sprouts up and grows — how, he himself does not know. The soil produces crops by itself; FIRST THE BLADE, THEN THE HEAD, THEN THE MATURE GRAIN IN THE HEAD. (Mk. 4:26-29)

We can see the various stages of the maturing and fruit-bearing process here. First, the blade, such as with a cornstalk, for example, sprouts out of the ground. Then, the blade develops into a stalk, which produces the head. Then, the grain (the fruit) forms on the head and develops unto full maturity. The plant itself must grow and mature first before it can produce the grain or bear the fruit. Thus, we see that maturity is indeed the fruit-bearing stage.

So also is it in the spiritual realm. As we mature into the Image of Christ, we will assuredly, eventually bear the fruit of the Kingdom of God. Spiritual fruitfulness, or the bearing of Godly fruit, is simply the natural produce of spiritual maturity.

The Pruning Process

However, there is another very important part of the fruit-bearing process which we need to discuss, which is "the pruning process." Jesus was alluding to this pruning process in His description of this fourth category of hearers, who He likened unto "good soil," saying that they bear fruit — "thirty, sixty, and a hundredfold."

We can see in this portion of what Jesus said concerning these hearers that there was an incremental, or we could even say, exponential, progressive increase in their capacity for bearing fruit. All of the hearers of this category bore fruit, and, indeed, as is emphasized in the parable as well as this book, they were the ONLY category of the four categories of hearers of the Word of God who did bear fruit. The very minimum amount of fruit this fourth category bore was a thirtyfold measure. That was the starting point. But, something caused their fruit production to increase from thirtyfold, to sixtyfold, and then finally to one-hundredfold productivity. As I have studied and re-studied this parable and its import for more than twenty-five years at the time of this writing, I have concluded that the reason for that exponential increase in productivity was "the pruning process" of the Lord.

In the following passage, Jesus alluded to and established the fact that our loving Heavenly Father, the Master Vinedresser, employs this pruning or perfecting process in our lives:

> "I am the true vine, and My father is the vinedresser. Every branch in Me that does not bear fruit, He takes away; and every branch that bears fruit, HE PRUNES IT, that it may bear more fruit." (Jn. 15:2)

In the natural, the capacity of trees and plants for bearing their particular fruit or flower, or whatever they produce, increases each season as they mature. Pruning before the fruit-bearing season, which is not the same for all plants and trees, further enhances that fruit-bearing capacity. The timing, how far back to cut, and so on, are all critical elements of the pruning process requiring preciseness, and are absolute requisites of the inveterate gardener's repertoire of expertise.

How cold, cruel, and compassionless it all appears, especially to the inexperienced, as the expert gardener wields his razor-sharp axe, summarily, swiftly, but shrewdly, severing from the tree what had been its glory, loveliness, and liveliness. What remains seems by comparison stark, crude, uncomely, and to portend of no other fate than inevitable, imminent death. Beyond that, how unnecessary and unreasonably radical such measures seem. But, again, that is only how it appears to the uninitiated, the untrained. The wise and knowledgeable gardener, however, knows by his years of experience that this pruning process, far from producing any adverse effects, will instead result in increased fruitfulness with each successive season.

The same is true in the spiritual realm in the lives of believers. When a believer does finally come to the place of maturity wherein he begins to bear some Kingdom fruit, there will come a season in which the Lord begins to do some "pruning" in the believer's life. This often comes as a great shock and surprise to many believers who are not prepared for it, chiefly because this pruning process is initiated *after* the initial fruit-bearing season. The gardener does not prune the plant until after its first fruit-bearing season, and in the case of some plants, after several seasons.

Likewise, it seems that it is not until a believer experiences his first season of bearing Kingdom fruit, that the Lord then begins to do some pruning, some cutting, some trimming back. When that happens, as with a tree or bush that has been pruned back before spring, which looks like it cannot possibly survive and that it will never bear fruit again, you may think you too cannot possibly survive the pain, the bewilderment, the disappointment, the discouragement, the self-doubt, the humiliation, and you may think you can never bear fruit again. Notwithstanding, though it may seem that way during the cold, dreary, barren days of winter, come spring, that tree will not only regrow its cropped branches, shoots, and foliage, but it will be more vibrant, viable, as well as fruitful during the next fruit-bearing season.

It is plain, at least to reasonable people, that the Master Vinedresser, especially in this last hour before the return of Christ, is in the process of pruning believers, both individually, as well as the collective Body of Christ. In some cases, He is cropping off dead, non-productive branches from the lives of individual believers and ministry organizations. But, even those who have experienced seasons of fruitfulness, He is pruning, but the reason, we must not forget, is so that that person or entity can bear more fruit:

> "Every branch in Me that does not bear fruit, He takes away; and every branch that bears fruit, He prunes it, THAT IT MAY BEAR MORE FRUIT." (Jn. 15:2)

The Bridegroom is coming soon to receive the Church as His Bride "without spot or wrinkle or any such thing." So, God is now preparing and purifying that Bride for the Wedding Supper of the Lamb. He is threshing the chaff from the life of every true believer. The winds which God allows to blow in our lives, blow the useless chaff away, and the useable true wheat of the Life of God falls to the threshing-floor and remains. Moreover, it is this grain of the Spirit which remains that distinguishes the true wheat from the hypocritical, deceptive tares.

Perseverance

There is yet one final, extremely vital, part of this process of bringing forth fruit that must be discussed, which is the requisite that once a believer has reached unto the fruit-bearing stage of maturity and has indeed begun to bring forth fruit of the Kingdom of God, that he or she continue in the face of many potent opposing forces to — persevere, persevere, persevere. In fact, Luke's rendition of this same Parable of the Sower concludes by explicitly delineating perseverance as the final requirement of the fruit-bearing process:

> And the seed in the good soil, these are the ones who have heard the word in an honest and good heart, and hold it fast, and bear fruit WITH PERSEVERANCE. (Lk. 8:15)

The Law of Perseverance is one of the foundational Laws of the Kingdom of God. Nothing of real value and permanence, including God's purposes for our lives, is ever accomplished "overnight," as the phrase goes, and without a strong measure of plain old dogged perseverance. Jesus said, "By your perseverance you will win your souls" (Lk. 21:19). Hebrews 6:12 tells us it is by faith AND PATIENCE that we inherit the promises of God. Hebrews 10:36 exhorts that we must persevere, "so that when you have done the will of God, you may receive what was promised."

There is just no such thing as instantaneous perfection. We all slip and stumble and experience momentary lapses, especially early on in our Christian walk. But, God giveth more grace! God does not boot us out of the Kingdom every time we make a mistake or stumble a little. If we confess our sins, He is faithful and just to forgive our sins, and to cleanse us from all unrighteousness (1 Jn. 1:9). If we confess our sins and failures, He does not impute them against us, which means He does not punish us for them or deploy measures to work against us as a result of those mistakes and misdeeds from which we have repented and sought forgiveness.

Contrary to what some people think, God is not hovering over us, just waiting for us to slip up so that He can kick us out of the Kingdom. No, He is doing everything He can to keep us *in* the Kingdom. He has made provision for our slip-ups and stumblings. If we will confess that we have sinned, and be willing to repent and remove the rock of sinful conduct we stumbled over, He will forgive it, justify us, and cleanse us from all the unrighteousness and defilement it has wrought in our lives.

This process of sanctification and purification is indeed a *process*, a process that just takes time, however, no matter how sincere, zealous, and earnest one may be. It is by no means instantaneous. It is a *walk*. In teaching an infant to walk, parents do not kick their baby out of the house and the family when they stumble and fall down, as they always do, over and over again. Instead, mother just picks baby up, brushes him off, stands him back on his feet, points him in the right direction, gives him a little pat of encouragement, and sends him off again towards his father, exhorting, "Walk to Daddy! Walk to Daddy!" And, off the kid goes again, tottering, slipping, and stumbling toward the goal of reaching Daddy. Indeed, that is just the way it is with believers as we walk toward our Father. We must forget what lies behind — all our faults, failures, and missteps — reach forward to what lies ahead, and press on toward the goal of the prize of the upward call of God in Christ Jesus (Plp. 3:13,14).

As we grow and progress in our life as a believer, it is a certainty and inevitability that we will encounter various temptations, tests, and trials (Jas. 1:2). But, we are to merely consider them all joy because of the knowledge that the testing of our faith will in the end produce perseverance, by which we will ultimately obtain the promises of God and reach our goal of bringing forth fruit, if we do not become discouraged and give up. If we will continue to persevere, then that perseverance will eventually bring about its perfect result, which is that we will "be perfect (mature) and complete, lacking in nothing" (Jas. 1:4).

The Seed of the Word of God will produce the fruit of the Kingdom in your life as you receive it in the good soil of acceptance and obedience. But, you must be patient, and continue to persevere in the face of adversity, faults, failures and mistakes. God will not give up on you as long as you will confess your sin when you stumble, ask Him to forgive you, do your best to turn away from those things, and continue to persevere. He *will* perfect you, but it will not happen instantaneously.

The experienced farmer knows there is a season for bringing forth fruit, even for the best of seed, planted in the best of soil. The crop will not come up overnight, but it *will* come up in due season. We must learn from him:

> Be patient, therefore, brethren, until the coming of the Lord. Behold, THE FARMER WAITS FOR THE PRECIOUS PRODUCE OF THE SOIL, being patient about it, until it gets the early and late rains. You too be patient; strengthen your hearts, for the coming of the Lord is at hand. (Jas. 5:7,8)

God is faithful. He will never quit on sincere believers whose hearts' desire is to be perfected in Him. "We are His workmanship" (Eph. 2:10). He is constantly working to make us into His "building" (1 Cor. 3:9) in conformity with the blueprint of His Image. Thus, we all need to continue to persevere, knowing and believing that eventually the Word of God *will* produce the fruit of the Kingdom of God in our life, if we faint not.

Conclusion

In the Parable of the Sower, Jesus indicated that this fourth category of hearers was the only category to bear fruit, and inherent in the parable is the procedure we must follow in order to become like "good ground" (KJV), and bear the fruit of the Kingdom of God in our own lives as God desires, intends, and even "ordained" (Jn. 15:16, KJV) us to bear. The following is a simple outline of that procedure:

STEP 1: Get up on the road of Eternal Life — by receiving Jesus Christ into your heart and life.

STEP 2: Remove the rocks of sinful conduct from your life — through genuine repentance.

STEP 3: Burn off the thorns of worldliness — through the sanctifying power of the Holy Spirit.

STEP 4: Receive, accept, and obey the Word and allow it to mature and sanctify you.

STEP 5: Allow the Lord to prune you.

STEP 6: Persevere, persevere, persevere.

This is the process for bearing the fruit of the Kingdom and Word of God. There are no short cuts. No step can be omitted. Follow this procedure step by step, continue to abide in Jesus and to allow His Word to abide in you, then you shall be one of those whom Jesus called "good soil," and you will eventually bear fruit thirty, sixty, and a hundredfold in your own life.

In so doing, you will be glorifying and exalting God the Father, and will prove yourself to be a true disciple and believer of the Lord Jesus Christ, for Jesus said, "By this is My Father glorified, that you bear much fruit, and so prove to be My disciples" (Jn. 15:8).

Moreover, when we shall see Him face to face, He shall say to you, "Well done, thou good and faithful servant…enter into the joy of your Master!"

Part Seven: The Imperativeness of Bringing Forth Fruit

Chapter Sixteen

The Litmus Test

The bearing of godly fruit is the "litmus test" of the true spiritual regeneration; that is, of whether or not a person has truly been Born Again. It is the test of true Christianity. Spiritual fruit is the "proof" of the New Birth. Jesus indicated it was incumbent upon all believers to bear much fruit, "and so PROVE to be My disciples."

The Apostle Paul spoke in terms of this "test" also, exhorting:

TEST yourselves to see if you are in the faith: EXAMINE yourselves! Or do you not recognize this about yourselves, that Jesus Christ is in you — unless indeed you fail THE TEST? (2 Cor. 13:5)

Paul tells us to "test," to "examine" *ourselves*. We should not wait for someone else to examine us, especially not the Lord. We should give *ourselves* the test. We should be continually examining *ourselves* to see if we pass the test of true salvation and regeneration.

In order to pass this crucial test, we must be proving through the evidence of our outward deeds that we are impregnated with the Life of Jesus Christ and His godly virtue within our spirit. If we have truly been Born Again by the Spirit of God, we should be demonstrating the character of God in our outward deeds.

The Greek word Paul used in the text quoted above that is translated as "fail the test" is "adokimos," which means to be disqualified and rejected by virtue of not passing the test for quality. Essentially, it means to be disapproved. It is the same root word Paul used in another passage in which he essentially exhorts believers to run the race of Christianity in accordance with the rules, lest after the race is completed we are then "disqualified" (1 Cor. 9:24-27).

Paul also exhorted believers to examine themselves in his instruction to the Corinthian church concerning the partaking of the Lord's supper, in order not to partake of it in an "unworthy manner": "But let a man EXAMINE himself, and so let him eat of the bread and drink of the cup" (1 Cor. 11:28). And then, in verse thirty-one he says that if we judge ourselves rightly in this manner, it will not be necessary for the Lord to judge us, assuming that we confess and repent from any iniquity that is realized.

Fruit Inspectors

In addition to judging our own lives for evidence of the fruit of righteousness, at times we must also make certain assessments and judgments concerning the spiritual condition of others, which is to say that at times we must be "fruit inspectors" who assay the fruit of others.

Of course, the Bible repeatedly warns us against judging others with condemnation. That is *"unauthorized* judgment." We don't cast stones of condemnation at others. We just examine their fruit. Fruit inspection is *"authorized* judgment."

The Bible also says, "he that is spiritual judgeth all THINGS, yet he himself is judged of no man" (1 Cor. 1:15, KJV). The key word in this passage is "THINGS." We are not to judge anyone's heart. Only God is authorized and able to do that rightly. The person of the Spirit does, however, judge all "THINGS," including the things people do, the things they say, and so on. Those "things" are their fruit, their works, their deeds.

We are to judge the fruit of others. Jesus taught us to identify whether people are good or bad by examining the fruit they bear, "for the tree is known by its fruit":

> Either make the tree good, and its fruit good; or make the tree bad, and its fruit bad; for the tree is known by its fruit...The good man out of his good treasure brings forth what is good; and the evil man out of his evil treasure brings forth what is evil. (Mat. 12:33-35)

Jesus Himself warned us to beware of the false brethren, hypocritical frauds, who would disguise themselves with the *outward* cloak of Christianity or spirituality, but who *inwardly* were carnal, satanically-ruled, "ravenous wolves." To *"be*-ware" of them, we must be *"a*-ware" of them and how to identify them. Jesus said we would be able to distinguish them "by their fruits":

> Beware of the false prophets, who come to you in sheep's clothing, but inwardly are ravenous wolves. You will know them BY THEIR FRUITS. Grapes are not gathered from thorn bushes, nor figs from thistles, are they? Even so, every good tree bears GOOD FRUIT; but the rotten tree bears BAD FRUIT. A good tree cannot produce bad fruit, nor can a rotten tree produce good fruit. Every tree that does not bear GOOD FRUIT is cut down and thrown into the fire. So then, YOU WILL KNOW THEM BY THEIR FRUITS. (Mat. 7:15-20)

Further evidence of this "authorized judgment" or "fruit inspection" can be found in the Apostle Paul's first letter to the Corinthians. One of the members of that church was known to be living in an incestual relationship with his father's wife (apparently, his step-mother). Paul was shocked and outraged at the report of such an abominable affair, and rebuked the entire church for their toleration of it.

In essence, he said that they should have already removed this person from their fellowship for having done such a deed. Then he says, "For I, on my part...have already JUDGED him who has so committed this" (1 Cor. 5:3). His discourse goes on to say that we are not to judge those outside of the church beyond determining they are indeed outside of the church by virtue of their deeds, but that we most certainly are to "judge those who are within the church" (1 Cor. 5:12). "But those who are outside, God judges," he said. Then, he charges them to: "Remove the wicked man from among yourselves" (1 Cor. 5:13) — which action required that the Corinthians make a specific judgment of that man on the basis of his own deeds.

In the subsequent chapter, he continues his discourse concerning the judgments made by believers, and asserts:

> Or do you not know that the saints will JUDGE the world? And if the world is JUDGED BY YOU, are you not competent to constitute the smallest law courts? Do you not know that we shall JUDGE angels? How much more matters of this life? (1 Cor. 6:2,3)

It only makes common sense that believers must at times make these assessments concerning the spiritual condition of others. Not in a "judgmental," condemning way. We are not to condemn others for their sin. We are to love them in spite of it. We can love the people with God's love, and still reject and disapprove of their sinful deeds. We are to leave the condemnation of others to God, the Supreme Judge.

Nevertheless, it is very necessary that we inspect the fruit of others. We must determine whether they are "good trees" or "bad trees," true "sheep" or "ravenous wolves" disguised in sheep's clothing. We are required to make those kind of judgments to prevent spiritual delusion and prevent spiritual injury to the sheep. In fact, we must do it to be able to correctly minister to others. Ministering to the unsaved as if they were saved would be doing them a grave injustice. Not reproving and restoring the backslidden would be just as bad. Even neglecting to rebuke those whose fruit indicate hypocrisy would be a great disservice to those persons.

Whatever the case may be, Jesus said we would be able to judge a person's spiritual condition by his or her fruit. It is necessary that we be "fruit inspectors." This is *authorized* judgment.

Fruitlessness Fails The Test

Any person who does not eventually bear forth the fruit of the Life and Kingdom of God fails the test of godliness. As James said, "faith, if it has no works (fruit), is dead, being by itself" (Jas. 2:17). Faith that does not produce the attesting fruits of the Spirit of God is not real. Real faith results in visible works which prove the validity of that faith. As the Living Bible says,

> ...it isn't enough just to have faith. You must also do good to prove that you have it. Faith that doesn't show itself by good works is no faith at all — it is dead and useless. (Jas. 2:17)

"Now wait just a minute," some religious people will say, "we are not saved by works, but by grace through faith that none should boast!"

Well, of course we are saved by grace through faith (Eph. 2:8). But, if we are truly saved, then our lives will naturally be producing the fruit of righteousness as evidence of our salvation, proving the validity of that faith through which we have been saved.

We know that salvation cannot be "earned" through so-called "good works." All such works in regards to obtaining rightstanding with God are but "filthy rags" (Is. 64:6) in His sight. Jesus Christ accomplished the only works acceptable to God for the salvation of mankind on the cross at Calvary. When He had completed His work, He cried out from that cursed tree, "It is finished." And it **WAS**! Our only "work" in regard to salvation is to *believe* in Jesus Christ, whom God hath sent to purchase our salvation (Jn. 6:29).

No, the works don't save you. Rather, fruit is the tangible proof that you indeed are saved. Outward works generated from inward qualities of godliness are the natural produce of salvation and redemption. True believers naturally produce good fruit from the Divine Nature that indwells them.

We are saved by grace through faith, but, as James contends, genuine faith will be producing good fruit, that is, works, deeds:

> What use is it, my brethren, if a man says he has faith, but he has no works? Can that faith save him?...Even so faith, if it has no WORKS, is dead, being by itself. But someone may well say, "You have faith, and I have WORKS; show me your faith *without* the WORKS, and I will show you my faith *by* my WORKS." You believe that God is one, You do well; the demons also believe, and shudder. But are you willing to recognize, you foolish fellow, that faith without works is useless? (Jas. 2:14-20; italics added)

Essentially, James asserts it is utterly foolish and futile to profess a faith in Jesus Christ that has no attesting fruit to prove it. He intimates that a faith that has no attesting works is not real, and thus cannot save anyone. Paraphrased, he says that a person who has attesting works could rightly say to one who professes a faith without works, "I can prove my faith *by* my works; let's see you prove yours *without* works!" As James' discourse goes on to indicate, such people with "fruitless faith" will often retort in defense, "Well, I believe in God." This "faith" they profess, however, is not real faith, but only mental assent to the existence of God. They do not have a personal relationship with God and know Him experientially. They just know "about" Him. To merely acknowledge that God exists is not real faith, but merely mental assent, concerning which James replies:

> You believe that there is one God. Good! Even the demons believe that — and shudder. (Jas. 2:19, NIV)

In other words, James is saying it is no great thing that you acknowledge the existence of God, for even the demons do that — none of the demons are athiests. They have the kind of "faith" which is based on mental assent. But, that "faith" certainly has not saved them. They now live in terror, awaiting their impending final judgment in the eternal fire of a real Hell.

Then, to support his case, James alludes to the examples of Abraham, when he offered up Isaac on the altar, and Rahab the harlot when she helped the Israelite spies to escape, as testimony to the fact that "a man is justified by works, and not by faith alone" (Jas. 2:24). From the case of Abraham he concludes, "You see that faith was working WITH HIS WORKS, and AS A RESULT OF THE WORKS, faith was perfected" (v. 22). And, from the case of Rahab he concludes, "for just as the body without the spirit is dead, so also FAITH WITHOUT WORKS IS DEAD" (v. 26).

Summarily then, any so called "faith" void of expression of the attributes of the Life of God in outward deeds is a dead, unreal, merely humanistic "faith." It amounts only to mental assent, and therefore cannot result in salvation or Eternal Life for anyone, "for with the HEART man believes" (Rom. 10:10). True faith is of the heart, or spirit, not the mind.

True faith is much like the wind — it is essentially manifest through its effects. When a person truly believes upon the Lord Jesus Christ and receives Him into His heart, an all-encompassing, ongoing process of spiritual transformation is effected. The spiritual death which has pervaded his entire being gives way to spiritual Life, the Life of God I limself, the Divine Nature. He is Born Again. He is "a new creature; the old things passed away; behold, new things have come" (2 Cor. 5:17).

The "new things" that come are the effects of that spiritual transformation process called "sanctification." They are the attributes of the Divine Nature of God Himself, which now permeate the innermost being of that regenerated person. Scripture calls these attributes "the fruit of the Spirit," which are: "love, joy, peace, patience, kindness, goodness, faithfulness, gentleness and self-control" (Gal. 5:22,23). These "fruits," or attributes of the Spirit, are manifest in the lives of true Born Again believers by virtue of the indwelling Holy Spirit. "Walking by the Spirit" causes them to be manifested in outward deeds.

No one is perfect, of course. Even though these fruits are within the spirit of believers, we do not always "walk by the spirit." We sometimes do indeed "walk by the flesh." Nevertheless, the general course of the person's life who has truly been Born Again will be manifesting the attributes of the Spirit indwelling him in outward deeds and behavior. Moreover, if we will practice walking by the Spirit, as time goes on, we will become more and more consistent at not "carry(ing) out the desire of the flesh" (Gal. 5:16).

Contrastingly, if these qualities are not eventually manifest in a generally consistent life style, it indicates that a real transformation of the heart by the indwelling of the Holy Spirit has not taken place. Persistent lack of godly fruit indicates the person is not Born Again, and is not a Child of God, but continues to abide in spiritual death, for "A tree is known by its fruit."

Bringing forth of good fruit is indeed "the litmus test" for whether or not a person is truly a Born Again child of God. And, probably no one summarizes the essence of that test better than the Apostle John:

> Little children, let no one deceive you; the one who PRACTICES RIGHTEOUSNESS is righteous, just as He is righteous; the one who PRACTICES SIN is of the devil; for the devil has sinned from the beginning. The Son of God appeared for this purpose, that He might destroy the works of the devil. No one who is born of God practices sin, because His seed abides in him; and he cannot sin, because he is born of God. By this the children of God and the children of the devil are obvious: anyone who does not PRACTICE RIGHTEOUSNESS is not of God, nor the one who does not love his brother. (1 Jn. 3:7-10)

People who persistently bring forth antithetical "bad fruit" fail the test and prove themselves "children of the devil," as John says. The "deeds of the flesh" are the antitheses of the "fruit of the Spirit." Paul identifies them thusly:

> Now the deeds of the flesh are evident, which are: immorality, impurity, sensuality, idolatry, sorcery, enmities, strife, jealousy, outbursts of anger, disputes, dissensions, factions, envying, drunkenness, carousing, and things like these, of which I forewarn you just as I have forewarned you that those who practice such things shall not inherit the kingdom of God. (Gal. 5:19-21)

In harmony with what John said concerning those who do not practice righteousness, the Apostle Paul bluntly declares that those who practice these fruit of unrighteouness — the deeds of the flesh — "shall not inherit the kingdom of God." He reiterated essentially the same verdict in his first letter to the Corinthians:

> Or do you not know that the unrighteous shall not inherit the kingdom of God? Do not be deceived; neither fornicators, nor idolaters, nor adulterers, nor effeminate, nor homosexuals, nor thieves, nor the covetous, nor drunkards, nor revilers, nor swindlers, shall inherit the kingdom of God. (1 Cor. 6:9,10)

Once again, in his letter to the Ephesians, Paul brazenly declares that people who practice such unrighteousness assuredly have no part in the Kingdom of God, and in fact shall only inherit God's wrath and judgment:

> For this you know with certainty, that no immoral or impure person or covetous man, who is an idolater, has an inheritance in the kingdom of Christ and God. Let no one deceive you with empty words, for because of these things the wrath of God comes upon the sons of disobedience. (Eph. 5:5,6)

Chapter Seventeen

Consequences of Barrenness

The Parable of the Sower is all about bringing forth fruit of the Kingdom of God, which is produced by the Seed of the Word of God when it is received in the "good soil" of a heart of yieldedness and obedience. Jesus gave us some tremendously enlightening insight into how this "mystery of the Kingdom" works. Any believer who will follow the procedure outlined in this powerful parable and explained in this book will bring forth fruit of the Kingdom of God in his or her own life. So effectual and infallible is this process that it is one of the few things in existence about which it can be correctly said, it is "guaranteed" to work; not just sometimes, in certain situations, merely for some people, but ALL the time, in ANY situation, for EVERYONE!

Now that we have dissected Jesus' paramount parable, examining the salient issues inherent within it, as well as delineated the specifics of the process by which a person can bear Kingdom fruit, one crucial aspect yet remains. I would be wholly remiss and derelict in my commission for writing this book if I ended it without addressing and admonishing regarding the absolute imperativeness of bringing forth the fruit of the Kingdom of God, as well as the sure and inevitable consequences for the failure thereof.

Most people, including the majority of professing Christians, simply do not understand and fully appreciate the imperativeness of bringing forth the fruit of Eternal Life and the Kingdom of God. At best, they seem to be of the mind that bearing fruit is optional, that it is nice if you do, but that it is not really mandatory. Yet, nothing could be further from the Truth. The consequences for not eventually bringing forth fruit of the Kingdom of God, which verify that a person has indeed been transferred from the kingdom of darkness into the Kingdom of Light, are extensive and fearsome.

We have already seen in the previous chapter what the Apostle Paul said about the possibility of failing the test (2 Cor. 13:5). A person not competing in accordance with the rules can be disqualified after finishing the race, allegorically speaking (1 Cor. 9:24-27). The rules of the race we are running require the practice of righteousness (1 Cor. 6:9,10, e.g.).

The practice of lawlessness results in disqualification from Eternal Life and being relegated to the unspeakable punishment of eternal death (Rev. 21:8, et al.). As we saw in the previous chapter, in both passages wherein Paul spoke of the "test" believers should give themselves to verify they are bona fide Christians, he used a Greek word connoting being rejected by virtue of not being able to pass the test for quality to describe those who did not meet the criteria. It means to be a "reject," a "castaway," a "reprobate."

Jesus Himself also spoke of such a final judgment of people who have professed to be believers but who demonstrated fruits of unrighteousness (Mat. 7:21-23). He said He would say to such people on the day of judgment, "I never knew you; depart from Me, you who practice lawlessness." These people also broke the rules, practicing "lawlessness," by violating God's Laws. They did not bring forth the fruits of righteousness, but rather the deeds of unrighteousness. Thus, they failed the test, and were rejected.

The weight of these Scriptures along with many others indicate the unequivocal and undeniable Truth that all those who do not bear the fruit of righteousness are "excluded from the Life of God" (Eph. 4:18), and will be excluded from Heaven and banished to the eternal fires of "the lake that burns with fire and brimstone" (Rev. 21:8) for eternal, unending judgment. I fully realize how grave, ominous, and even odious to some such an assessment and statement is, especially to ears that are accustomed only to being tickled by modernistic, so-called "positive preaching" so prevalent today, which denies or ignores the truth of Divine judgment. But, it is nonetheless precisely what the Word of God declares. I did not write the Bible; **God** did! I'm just reporting what it says. It is vital that we do not "sugarcoat" the Word of God, for it is the eternal destiny of us all that is at stake.

John The Baptist certainly did not sugarcoat the Word of God. He unabashedly preached a baptism of repentance for the forgiveness of sins, admonishing it was necessary to "bring forth fruit in keeping with your repentance" (Mat. 3:8). He also made it abundantly clear that bringing forth of such fruit was by no means optional, but rather, failure to bring forth fruit would result in eternal judgment:

> And the axe is already laid at the root of the trees; every tree therefore that does not bear good fruit is cut down and thrown into the fire. (Mat. 3:10)

Jesus also trumpeted forth essentially the same dire and severe warning: "Every tree that does not bear good fruit is cut down and thrown into the fire" (Mat. 7:19). He again referred to this same final judgment for not bearing fruit in His discourse regarding the Vine and the Branches:

> If anyone does not abide in Me, he is thrown away as a branch, and dries up; and they gather them, and cast them into the fire, and they are burned. (Jn. 15:6)

Just so there is no possibility of misunderstanding, let me state categorically in direct opposition to the ludicrous argumentations made by devoid of the Spirit, purported "theologians" who attempt to "explain away" the matter of Divine retribution and even Hell itself, that all these references of being "thrown into the fire" are metaphorical references to "eternal punishment" (Mat. 25:46) in which those who have been rejected and disqualified from Eternal Life are cast into a very literal "lake of fire," which is Hell (Mat. 25:41-46; Rev. 20:11-15; 21:8; et al.).

Judgment Begins With Believers

You see, nearly two thousand years ago, the Apostle Peter wrote, "It is time for judgment to begin with the household of God" (1 Pet. 4:17). If it was "time for judgment to begin" way back then — it certainly is "high time" now. The rarely understood Truth is that God's judgment actually begins with the judgment of believers.

Further corroboration of that Truth is found in the message of John The Baptist, who many years before Peter wrote his words, said that God's winnowing fork was in His hand, and He had already commenced then the process of cleaning out His threshing floor, the end of which will be that "He will gather His wheat into the barn, but He will burn up the chaff with unquenchable fire" (Mat. 3:12). That process continues yet today. God is separating the true wheat (i.e., true believers) from the tares (i.e., false brethren) according to their own fruit and deeds. "The end of the age" is quickly closing in upon us, and the fruitless tares are being gathered into piles for burning, while the real grain-bearing wheat is being gathered into the barn (Mat. 13:24-40).

Indeed, judgment has already begun with the household of God, and those who are real wheat are becoming more and more distinguished from those who are mere tares. And, as Jesus said, the true identifier distinguishing the fruit from the tares is the fruit, or produce, of the plant.

Barren Lives

Tares, as already mentioned, are virtually identical to true wheat, except that it does not bear any fruit or grain. The barren fig tree, which Jesus cursed when He found it was barren of fruit (Mat. 21:18,19), is another allegory Jesus evoked to exemplify professing Christians whose lives are barren of fruit. It was a hypocritical tree because, though it was the fruit-bearing season and its green leaves portended of fruit, it had none. Jesus discovered the tree was barren when He approached it to pick some figs to satisfy His hunger. The hypocritical barrenness of this tree angered Jesus, and caused Him to curse it, which is to say He pronounced judgment upon it. Matthew recounts the effect was instantaneous, "And at once the fig tree withered."

Jesus demonstrated in the case of this barren fig tree that He utterly despised hypocrisy. But the story of this fruitless tree is not recorded in Holy Writ merely to testify of Jesus' disdain of barren fig trees. Rather, the barren fig tree was emblematic of the lives of barren people, and the incident appears in Scripture to illustrate Jesus' abhorrence of the hypocrisy of people who purport to know God, but whose lives are barren of Kingdom fruit.

Jesus also demonstrated His contempt for hypocrisy with His utter denunciation of the Pharisees for their religious hypocrisy (Mat. 23:1-33). Like the fig tree Jesus cursed and the Pharisees He denounced because of their hypocritical barrenness, there will come the day when those who have professed to be believers but failed to bring forth the fruit of Eternal Life will have judgment pronounced upon them. "Hypocrites," "false brethren," "tares," "deceitful workers," are some of the appellations God, in His Word, attributes to hypocritical people who purport to know and serve Him, but whose lives are barren of Kingdom fruit.

We have just discussed the actual historical *incident* involving a barren fig tree. Jesus also illustrated His complete disdain for hypocritical barrenness in a *parable* of a barren fig tree:

> And He began telling this parable: "A certain man had a fig tree which had been planted in his vineyard; and he came looking for fruit on it, and did not find any. And he said to the vineyard-keeper, 'Behold, for three years I have come looking for fruit on this fig tree without finding any. Cut it down! Why does it even use up the ground?' And he answered and said to him, 'Let it alone, sir, for this year too, until I dig around it and put in fertilizer; and if it bears fruit next year, fine; but if not, cut it down.'" (Lk. 13:6-9)

This parable illustrates the little understood fact that there comes a time when even God Himself will be looking for fruit in a person's life. The owner of the vineyard, who symbolized God, came looking for fruit on the tree for three consecutive years after it had grown to the fruit-bearing stage. But, the tree was barren. The vineyard owner had allowed more than ample time for it to begin bearing fruit, but it continued to be fruitless year after year.

Consequently, the angry owner gave the order for the barren tree to be cut down, so as to no longer take up valuable ground. But the vineyard-keeper, who symbolized ministers, interceded for the fig tree, which represented members of the Body of Christ. He asked the vineyard-owner to allow him to dig up the ground around the tree, which was emblematic of the soil of the believer's heart, and to put in some fertilizer, symbolizing the Word of God, and allow the tree to remain in the vineyard for one more year. Then, if it still did not bear fruit after that year had passed, the vineyard-keeper would concede and carry out the vineyard-owner's command to cut it down.

God-appointed ministers truly knowledgeable of their Scriptural responsibilities to the Body of Christ have sometimes found themselves in the unfortunate situation portrayed in this parable. There comes a time when a professing believer who has persisted in bearing no godly fruit but has instead persistently brought forth the fruit of unrighteousness, needs to be reproved, rebuked, and subsequently even removed from the local body of which he is a part if he does not repent. This is the responsibility of the God-appointed shepherds in the Body of Christ.

The Lord is so merciful and forbearing, but after a period of time, God expects believers to begin to bear some fruit consistent with His Life. After what God in His infinite and perfect knowledge considers an ample time for fruit to be brought forth has elapsed, God Himself will "come looking for fruit," according to Jesus' parable. When He has come year after year looking for fruit in a person's life "without finding any," He may soon give the command to the minister, as He did in this parable to the vineyard-keeper, to "Cut it down!"

Now the initial reaction of a true shepherd who is truly "moved by compassion" to care for the sheep of God's Flock to God's command to cut down the tree, will be like that of the vineyard-keeper in the parable. He will be compelled to intercede for the person he has been diligently caring for and in whose spiritual well-being he has invested considerable time and energy. Also, he will beseech the Lord for additional time in order to "dig around," or plow up the soil of the person's heart with some forthright reproof and exhortation, as well as to "put in fertilizer" of additional teaching of the Word of God.

And then, if, after an ample period of time to allow for repentance and restoration, the person still does not bear some Kingdom fruit as evidence of being a true child of God, then the shepherd will reluctantly concede and comply with the Lord's command to remove the offender (1 Cor. 5:13), not from the Kingdom of God, of course, for only God has that power, but from the fellowship of the saints, until such time the offender repents and seeks restoration.

Nevertheless, though human shepherds only remove persistent offenders from the fellowship of other believers (i.e., the local church), those who do not eventually repent from their waywardness will at their final judgment find themselves excluded from eternal fellowship with God as well (Gal. 5:19-21; Eph. 5:3-6; et al.). The propitiatory sacrifice of Jesus Christ does not extend to those who "go on sinning willfully AFTER RECEIVING THE KNOWLEDGE OF THE TRUTH" (Heb. 10:22). God will not forever tolerate persistent willful, sinful conduct by professing believers who have had ample time to repent, but have refused to do so.

There is much Scripture to support this assertion, far too many passages to delineate here, but a prime example that will suffice for our purposes here is the Lord's condemnation of the church at Thyatira for their continued toleration of immoral and idolatrous activity among their members. Their rebellion was being induced by a rebellious and insubordinate woman, who, in violation of the Lord's explicit command that women are not permitted to teach or be in authority over men, was both teaching and leading in this church:

> But I have this against you, that you tolerate the woman Jezebel, who calls herself a prophetess, and she TEACHES AND LEADS My bondservants astray, so that they commit acts of immorality and eat things sacrificed to idols. And I GAVE HER TIME TO REPENT: AND SHE DOES NOT WANT TO REPENT OF HER IMMORALITY. Behold, I will cast her upon a bed of sickness, and those who commit adultery with her into great tribulation, unless they repent of their deeds. And I will kill her children with pestilence; and all the churches will know that I am He who searches the minds and hearts; and I will give to each one of you according to your deeds. (Rev. 2:20-23)

Jesus' condemnation of the Pergamum church, likewise for immorality and unauthorized teaching, was similar:

> But I have a few things against you, because you have there some who hold the teaching of Balaam, who kept teaching Balak to put a stumbling block before the sons of Israel, to eat things sacrificed to idols, and to commit acts of immorality. Thus you also have some who in the same way hold the teaching of the Nicolaitans. Repent therefore; or else I am coming to you quickly, and I will make war against them with the sword of My mouth. (Rev. 2:14-16)

Even now, Jesus, as the Head of the Church, is coming to "make war" with such people who refuse to repent, with "the sword of (His) mouth," which is the Word of God, spoken through His anointed and appointed ministers. God is going to judge the churches and their shepherds who have tolerated evil members and not removed them as He has commanded (1 Cor. 5:13, et al.). God's charge to Ezekiel extends unto every shepherd:

> Son of man, I have appointed you a watchman...whenever you hear a word from My mouth, warn them from Me. When I say to the wicked, "You shall surely die"; and you do not warn the wicked from his wicked way that he may live, that wicked man shall die in his iniquity, BUT HIS BLOOD I WILL REQUIRE AT YOUR HAND. Yet if you have warned the wicked, and he does not turn from his wickedness or from his wicked way, he shall die in his iniquity; but you have delivered yourself. (Ezk. 3:17-19)

The Body of Christ is just going to have to wake up to the harsh and unfortunate realization that not everyone who calls himself a Christian is a true Born Again child of God. Satan has infiltrated our fellowships with his counterfeits, who disguise themselves as "angels of light" (1 Cor. 11:14,15).

There really are "wolves in sheep's clothing" (Mat. 7:15). There really are "castaways" who have been disqualified from the prize (1 Cor. 9:27), and people who have fallen away from the faith to which they once adhered (1 Tim. 4:1). We must realize that these things are true and not merely religious fables or metaphors. Indeed, there really are spiritual frauds like those Jesus described in the parable of the tares, in which He alludes once again to the consequential judgment for barrenness:

> Another parable put he forth unto them, saying, The kingdom of heaven is likened unto a man which sowed good seed in his field: but while men slept, his enemy came and sowed tares among the wheat, and went his way. But when the blade was sprung up, and BROUGHT FORTH FRUIT, THEN APPEARED THE TARES ALSO. So the servants of the householder came and said unto him, Sir, didst not thou sow good seed in the field? from whence then hath it tares? He said unto them, An enemy hath done this. The servants said unto him, Wilt thou then that we go and gather them up? But he said, Nay; lest while ye gather up the tares, ye root up also the wheat with them. Let both grow together until the harvest; and in the time of the harvest I will say to the reapers, Gather ye together first the tares, and BIND THEM IN BUNDLES TO BURN THEM; but gather the wheat into my barn. (Mat. 13:24-30, KJV)

There are several points in this parable relevant to our topic of discussion here. First, He said that it was "while men slept" that the enemy, which was symbolic of Satan, stealthily infiltrated his tares in among the wheat. Some people foolishly contend that we do not need to be concerned with what the devil is doing, and that we should merely ignore him and all his devices. That is "hogwash!" The Bible plainly tells us not to be ignorant of Satan's schemes (strategic battle plans) "in order that no advantage be taken of us by Satan" (2 Cor. 2:11). The Body of Christ needs to wake up and quit sleeping while the enemy uncontestedly infiltrates the Church with hoards of barren frauds.

A second truth Jesus reveals in this parable is that the tares only became evident and distinguishable from the real wheat when the wheat "brought forth fruit," in contrast to the barrenness of the tares. Tares are useless weeds which look virtually identical to wheat. The only difference is that tares have absolutely no grain, or fruit, on the stalk as does real wheat. Tares are counterfeits. Jesus taught us, "You will know them by their fruits" (Mat. 7:30). Thus, we can distinguish the tares from the wheat by whether or not there is any fruit.

Tares are the natural enemy of wheat. If allowed to grow unchecked in a field of wheat, tares will either choke out the wheat crop or at the very least seriously impair its yield. So it is also with the false brethren Satan surreptitiously sows in our fellowships, if allowed to grow unchecked, they can bring serious spiritual injury to that body, especially to fledgling and less mature believers.

But, in the end, according to the parable, the true wheat of God's Field or Kingdom will be separated from the barren tares. The tares will be gathered into piles for burning, and the real wheat will be gathered into God's barn for eternal fellowship with Jesus.

Jude aptly described these false brethren with their ungodly, barren lives, and the judgment that awaits them:

> These men are those who are hidden reefs in your love feasts when they feast with you without fear, caring for themselves; clouds without water, carried along by winds; autumn trees WITHOUT FRUIT, DOUBLY DEAD, uprooted; wild waves of the sea, casting up their own shame like foam; wandering stars for whom the black darkness has been reserved forever. (Jude 12,13)

In the final analysis, bringing forth fruit is what the Parable of the Sower is all about. Jesus reveals in it the step-by-step process believers must follow in order to bring forth the fruit of the Kingdom of God. Moreover, what has been established unequivocally in this chapter is the fact that bearing Godly fruit is an absolute Divine imperative, as well as the incontrovertible fact that the consequences of failure to bear Kingdom-fruit is disqualification from "the race" to attain the prize of Eternal Life and eternal fellowship with God.

Part Eight: Epilogue

Chapter Eighteen

Savior to Judge

The Parable of the Sower is all about bringing forth fruit. Bringing forth fruit is not optional, but imperative. The consequence for not bringing forth fruit is eternal judgment. That is as succinctly as it can be said, and certainly the case has been well corroborated within this volume. Still, some people will want to quarrel with these statements and conclusions concerning judgment, saying, "How could a God who is Love send people to Hell for eternal judgment?" Others will recite such passages as: "God sent not His Son into the world to condemn it, but that the world through Him would be saved."

Well, certainly God is Love, and Jesus did indeed come into the world to save all who will believe in and obey Him, not to condemn them. Moreover, God's hand is outstretched to all mankind, beckoning them to turn away from sin and self, and to turn to Him. Jesus came to offer salvation rather than judgment to the world. Nevertheless, it is also a certainty that The Day of the Lord — the time when this same God of Love will exercise the Divine Judgment and pour out the Divine Wrath which until now He has held in abeyance — is close at hand.

I once heard a true story that powerfully illustrates all this and puts it all in proper perspective.

A very young boy was once swimming in a lake, and carelessly wandered out into the very deep water, far away from shore. Soon his young, underdeveloped muscles became tired, and he began struggling to swim. Very quickly the frantic struggle was to merely stay afloat and keep his head above water. Realizing he was drowning the now fatigued and frightened youngster began crying out for help. Immediately, upon hearing his desperate cries, a man who had been lounging on the shore, dove into the water, swam out to the boy, locked his arms around him, and pulled him safely to shore. This man, who the boy did not know, had very literally saved the boy's life. How ecstatically grateful was the lad toward that man for saving his life, which gratefulness he expressed profusely and repeatedly through many tears.

Afterward, life just sort of went on, and the boy never saw the man again.

In the passage of time, as the young boy grew first into adolescence and then into adulthood, he began to rebel and to get into trouble over and over again, until finally when he had become a young man, he robbed a bank and in the process shot and killed someone. No longer was this a matter of "juvenile delinquency" for which he would merely receive a few days of retention and then be sent home in the custody of his parents. Now, he could be sentenced to death for having taken someone else's life. Though externally he had always presented a macho, tough-guy image, he now was truly petrified inside.

On the first day of the trial, the young man walked into the courtroom and sat down. Soon, the bailiff cried out to everyone in the courtroom, "All rise!" Then, to the young man's utter astonishment, the robed man who strode through the door, the man who would be his judge, in whose hands his fate would rest, was none other than the man who had saved his life so many years before. A ripple of relief and delight shuddered through the young man's body as he contemplated the great fortune he had encountered in having as his *judge* the man who so many years before had been his *savior*.

As the trial progressed, with the prosecutor presenting the case that the young man was a murderer and should be put to death as punishment for his law-breaking, and his defense attorney attempting to spare his life, the young man began to develop a cocky confidence. Even if he was found guilty, there was no way, he thought, that this kind, merciful man who had once put his own life on the line to become the youngster's savior and save his life, would ever sentence him to death.

Consequently, the young man was totally unprepared for what ensued on the final day in the courtroom.

After the jury had heard all the evidence in the case and deliberated the verdict, court was reconvened. "Has the jury reached a verdict, and if so, what is that verdict," the judge queried the foreman. "We have, your Honor," replied the foreman. "We, the jury, find the defendant **guilty** as charged of murder in the first degree." Remarkably, the young man remained unconcerned as he was taken back to his cell to await sentencing by the judge.

Soon the judge ordered court to be reconvened. As he entered the courtroom for the final time, the bailiff once again cried out, "All rise!" and ordered the defendant forward to stand before the judge. With a catch in his throat and tears welling up in his eyes, the inveterate jurist began, "Young man, based on all the evidence that has been presented in this courtroom on which basis a jury has found you guilty of the charge of murder in the first degree, I have no choice, based on the laws governing this court, but to sentence you to death as the penalty for your lawless deeds!"

In total shock, incredulity, and terror, the young man screamed out, "But, sir, don't you remember — a few years ago you saved my life, and now are you sentencing me to death?"

With obvious agony and sadness, and tears trickling down his face, the judge replied, "Yes, son, I remember ever so well saving you that day years ago. But, you see, son, **then** I was your *savior*; **today**, I am your *judge.*"

Jesus Christ is now our *Savior*, but just as sure as the sun rises in the east, a day will come when He will be our *Judge*:

> Therefore having overlooked the times of ignorance, God is now declaring to men that all everywhere should repent, because HE HAS FIXED A DAY IN WHICH HE WILL JUDGE THE WORLD THROUGH A MAN WHOM HE HAS APPOINTED, having furnished proof to all men by raising Him from the dead. (Acts 17:30,31)

I beg all those reading these words to make a complete and final surrender of your life unto the Lord Jesus Christ as your personal Savior now, while He is the *Savior*, before this same Jesus becomes your *Judge*.

If you have never done that, or if you have backslidden from your relationship with Jesus, or if you once had confessed Jesus as your Savior and have since fallen away from Him, please pray this prayer with me and mean it with all your heart:

> Dear Lord Jesus, I am a sinner. I have sinned against you in thought, word, and deed. I desperately need a Savior. I believe you are the only Savior of all mankind I believe you died for me on an old rugged Cross nearly two thou-sand years ago to pardon my sin. I am sorry for my sin and I want to be forgiven of all the ways in which I have transgressed against you. I confess my sinfulness to you. I confess I am powerless to help myself or to save myself. I need you to help me and save me. I call upon you now as my Lord, Master, and Savior. Though I do not deserve it, on the basis of grace and through faith in you, I ask you to cleanse me from all my sin, and to forgive me. I ask you to receive me into your love and fellowship and Kingdom. Love me, Lord, and help me to love you. Come into my heart and live there forever. In the name of Jesus I pray. Amen.

Now, my friend, if you prayed that prayer and meant it with all your heart, on the authority of God's Holy Word, I declare unto you: Your sins are forgiven and washed in the blood of the Lamb. You are saved from the wrath and judgment of God. Jesus now lives on the inside of you in the form of the Holy Spirit. Heaven is now your home, and you are now a member of the Holy Race and Kingdom of God! You are now a Born Again Child of God, a joint-heir with Jesus Christ!

Now go and make a public profession of your faith to someone; if possible, someone you know to be a true believer in Christ. Tell them you gave your life to Jesus Christ and were Born Again. Jesus said, if we would confess Him before *men*, He would confess us before the *Father* in Heaven. Also, Gods tell us in His Word that **confessing** Christ Jesus as Lord and Savior with our *mouth* is necessary in order to be saved, in addition to **believing** in our *heart*:

> But what does it say? "The word is near you, in your *mouth* and in your *heart*" — that is the word of faith which we are preaching, that if you **CONFESS with your MOUTH** Jesus as Lord, **AND BELIEVE in your HEART** that God raised Him from the dead, YOU SHALL BE SAVED; for with the *HEART* man BELIEVES, resulting **righteousness** (rightstanding) with God, and **with the *MOUTH* he CONFESSES**, resulting in **SALVATION** (Rom. 10:8-10).

Get yourself a Bible, and start reading it, beginning with the Gospel of John.

You will also have a desire to become a part of a local church-family. Search out a Bible-believing, devil-chasing, Holy Ghost-baptism-believing church to attend. Tell the minister you've given your life to the Lord. Doing it will bless you, and it will give your brothers and sisters in Christ an opportunity to rejoice along with the angels of Heaven because one more sinner has turned from sin, and surrendered to Jesus! Then, allow your church-family to love you and help you to grow in the Lord.

Welcome to the Family of God, Dear Child of God! Welcome!

One more thing, be sure to read this book many times and keep it handy for reference to keep reminding yourself of all the things you've learned through it concerning the Mystery of the Kingdom of God and how to bear the fruit of the Kingdom of God in your own life. Put all the principles Jesus taught us in the Parable of the Sower into practice each and every day of your life!

If you do, you will one day hear the Master say to you, "Well, done, thou good and faithful servant; you were faithful with a few things, I will put you in charge of many things; enter into the joy of your Master" (Mat. 25:23).

www.ingramcontent.com/pod-product-compliance
Lightning Source LLC
Chambersburg PA
CBHW032122090426
42743CB00007B/428